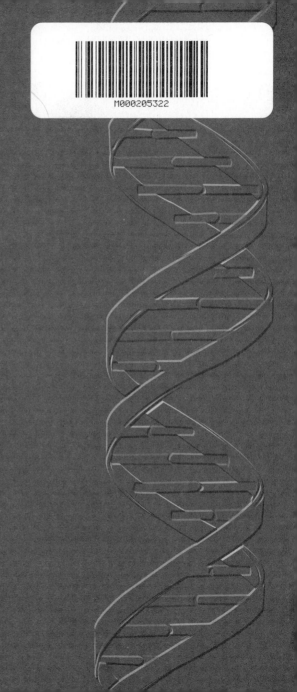

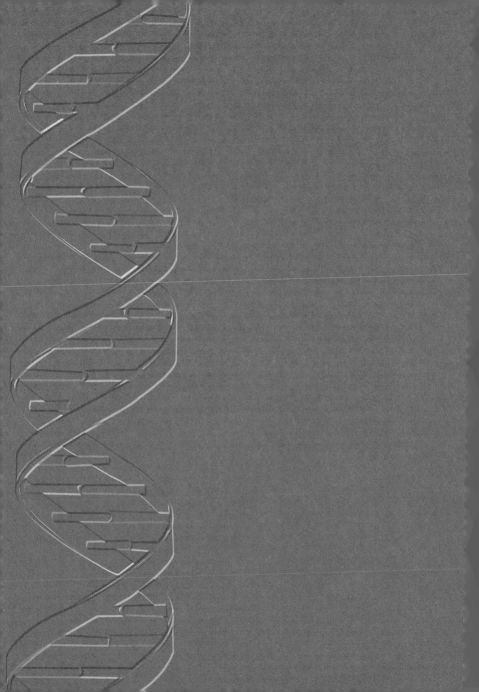

Praise for previous "Crazy Wisdom" editions . . .

"The missing link between sit-down meditation and stand-up comedy."
PAUL KRASSNER, FOUNDER AND EDITOR OF
THE REALIST

"[A] wild, esoteric excursion."
BOOKLIST

"Deeply wise . . . wonderfully insightful; and delightfully humorous."
THE UTNE READER

"A dim sum feast of perceptive and amusing morsels. Nisker succeeds in fashioning an original pattern from motley patches of wisdom."
SAN FRANCISCO CHRONICLE

"Ah the foolishness of the real! This is good medicine."
GARY SNYDER, PULITZER PRIZE—WINNING POET

"A rich and subtle tradition, universal and yet elusive, is fully explored. . . . Written in the unique voice of a Buddhist, social activist, and satirist, it is a delight to read."

FRITJOF CAPRA, AUTHOR OF *THE TAO OF PHYSICS*

"When that rascal-ly fellow Scoop points an idiot finger at Ultimate Truth, what else to do but laugh?"

RAM DASS, SPIRITUAL TEACHER AND AUTHOR OF *BE HERE NOW*

. . . and for other books by Wes "Scoop" Nisker

"[Buddha's Nature is] a milestone in contemporary Buddhism. I dare you to find a book on science that is so personal, or a book on meditation that is so funny and forgiving."

JOANNA MACY, AUTHOR OF *WORLD AS LOVER, WORLD AS SELF*

"Buddha's Nature is truly a healing and historic achievement."

BRIAN SWIMME, AUTHOR OF *THE UNIVERSE STORY*

"[The Big Bang, the Buddha, and the Baby Boom is] wry, hip, fast, breezy. . . . Nisker's romp is a tender triumph."

PUBLISHERS WEEKLY

To Susan –
Stay wise

Crazy Wisdom

Saves the

World Again!

I get crazier!

Blessings –

Wes

Wes "Scoop" Nisker

Crazy Wisdom Saves the World Again!

Handbook for a
Spiritual Revolution

Featuring "The Evolution Sutra"
and "Be Here Wow!"

Stone Bridge Press   •   Berkeley, California

Published by
Stone Bridge Press, Inc.
P. O. Box 8208, Berkeley, CA 94707
TEL 510-524-8732 • sbp@stonebridge.com • www.stonebridge.com

A Cody's Book is a collaborative imprint of Stone Bridge Press, Inc. and Cody's Books, Inc., Berkeley, California.

Printed in the United States of America.

10 9 8 7 6 5 4 3 2 1   2012 2011 2010 2009 2008

LIBRARY OF CONGRESS CATALOGING-IN-PUBLICATION
Nisker, Wes.
  Crazy wisdom saves the world again! : handbook for a spiritual revolu-
tion : featuring "the Evolution sutra" / Wes "Scoop" Nisker.
      p. cm.
    ISBN 978-1-933330-69-3 (pbk.)
    1. Spiritual life. I. Title.
    BL624.N57 2008
    204—dc22
                                    2008007837

Contents

Acknowledgments

I would like to acknowledge and give thanks to those who made this book possible, including the DNA molecules, mitochondria, all earthlings (especially the denizens of the plant and animal kingdoms), the earth itself, the Holocene epoch (interglacial), Turtle Island (the continent I live on), the Shasta bioregion, Berkeley, most definitely my family and friends, and, of course, the mystery that lies within/beneath/behind it all. I couldn't have written this book without you.

Crazy Wisdom Saves the World Again!

1

A Message from the Department of Crazy Wisdom

"The new world is not only possible, she is on her way. When I am quiet I can hear her breathing."
ARUNDHATI ROY

Future humans may look back at us with wonder, or maybe disdain. They will see how we wasted so much of our energy and genius on ancient tribal wars, silly religious disputes, and basic gluttony, when all the while our planet's life support systems were collapsing around us. Perhaps the future humans—who may be *Homo sapiens sapiens sapiens*, or the next wiser ones—will bring us to trial in absentia for the holocaust of species that went on in our time—the biocide. We will be indicted for crimes against *non-humanity*.

Research shows that we are in the middle of the fifth or sixth largest species die-off in biological history. The naturalists call it an "extinction spasm," which conjures an image of the earth itself convulsing as it tries to shake off an infestation of some unhealthy organisms. I wonder who they could be?

Recently I read an article in the back pages of the *San Francisco Chronicle* under the headline "Humans' Basic Needs Destroying Planet Rapidly." (The front page of that day's *Chronicle* was of course devoted to more important stories.) The article cites the results of a four-year United Nations study, "The Millennium Ecosystem Assessment," which found that humans have "ruined approximately 60 percent of earth's ecological systems to meet our demands for food, fresh water, timber and fuel." We have discovered a problem, and it is us.

What is going on?! Why are we screwing things up so badly on our planet? Could this be what nature wants? Maybe we are competing with the conscious life on other planets to see who can survive the longest, and the winner gets a big prize. If our earth team is going to win, or if we humans simply want to survive for a little while longer, we had better wake up and smell the CO_2. The wolf is now at the door, stopping by on its way to extinction.

When I reflect on our predicament, I think, "We have to do everything in our power to stop the destruction of the earth's life support systems." At the same time, part of me says, "We have to learn to let it all go." It sounds paradoxical, but I live with that dilemma, just as I assume others do in this post-postmodern world. We are aware of the disaster that is taking place on earth, and at the same time we have knowledge of hundreds of billions of solar systems like our own. Are we overdramatizing our human existence? Are we too sentimental about life on earth?

The discoveries of Western science reveal that we are at the mercy of massive streams of cosmic and biological evolution, forces that couldn't care less about our desire to survive as a species, let alone our hope of creating justice and peace. Can we expect to have any significant influence on the length of time that life will continue to evolve on this tiny little rock hurtling through space? As the Taoist sage Chuang Tzu once asked, "Do you really think you can take over the universe and improve it?"

What resolves the dilemma for us is Mother Nature herself, who boldly writes out directions for us in our DNA, the primary command being simple: "Survive!" We are built to struggle for survival, however we come to envision the necessary action, because that's just the way we are built. You *must* try to save yourself, and that means trying to save the world!

Ironically, for all of previous human history our survival instinct had us spending our time and energy trying to protect ourselves from nature, and now suddenly we are called on to protect nature from us.* Some would say we are lucky to have a planetary crisis like this on our watch. As my eco-Buddhist activist friend Joanna

---

* But of course we *are* nature, so who is leading this dance anyway?

Macy says, "Rejoice! Opportunities to become a bodhisattva (a Buddhist saint of compassion) are extremely plentiful right now!" I draw on more mundane motivations, which include, "What else is there to do?" I mean, what are your choices? You can either try to keep yourself stimulated with the latest toys of our civilization or work to change the course of history: you can either try to stay apace with the endless flow of your desires or help undermine the juggernaut of destruction, the "*self-consumption*" economy.

Each of us has our own temperament and talent and has to decide how best to use them, but everybody can do something to help the cause. Just thinking subversive thoughts is a good start: Try to imagine other ways to organize an economy. Picket in front of an oil company of your choice. Go to the ocean (the primal amniotic fluid) and chain yourself to an endangered coral reef. Since part of our challenge is to bring the divine back home again, you might want to get involved in some regular pagan ritual. Go ahead and hug a tree, or bow down and kiss the earth. The age of cynicism is dead!

One big problem is that there are just too many of

us. I recently saw a bumper sticker that said, "Six billion people can't be right." Maybe those who wrote the Bible got the proclamation wrong: It wasn't "Go forth and multiply." It was "Go forth and *add*." The Dalai Lama said that the solution is to ordain more monks and nuns.

* * * * *

I have a practical suggestion for the politicians in Washington, D.C. Over the past few years they have tried to create a new intelligence agency, with a "czar" who would coordinate whatever intelligence our agencies manage to find. But what the United States really needs is a department of *wisdom*, a government agency staffed by philosophers, anthropologists, historians, some jesters, and even a few mystics: people who see the world in a different way from economists, generals, and senators. Although the political right may currently be in charge, our real oppressor is the "left-brain" government. A department of wisdom just might provide some critical balance of powers.

If I were in the department of wisdom, I would call for an immediate moratorium on progress, to last at least a half-century. We had a whole lot of progress in the last couple of centuries, and although it brought us pain-killing drugs, space telescopes, and Velcro®, it appears we can no longer keep up with our own ingenuity. We now race madly around in our individual boxes of steel, chasing after satisfaction, and in the process we are throwing the atmosphere out of whack by burning up two or three geological epochs worth of the sun's stored energy in one great choking bonfire of the vanities. We have spent the better part of our genius figuring out new ways to blow each other up or learning how to go faster, and in our fear and haste we forgot about who we are and where we are going. We need to relax, deeply, and let our hearts and minds catch up with our tool-making ability, which has gotten way "out of hand." What we need is a century of less doing and more "being." The next revolution is a big slowdown.

I also have some broad suggestions on how we might help heal our sick civilization and the ailing planet, based on the understanding of crazy wisdom, a long-running tradition of tricksters, saints, philosophers, self-proclaimed fools, and other disreputable characters. Rather than practical solutions, crazy wisdom offers a stance, an attitude to carry with us as we proceed through these ominous days.*

First and foremost, keep a big perspective in your pocket, ready to be unfurled in your head at a moment's notice. The big perspective is your spiritual juice, the view-glue that connects you to everything else and inspires both your effort and humility. It reminds us that we are working on a long-term project here, and to not measure success according to election cycles or decades or even centuries. Life has been working on this survival issue for at least three and a half billion years, and it's always managed to find a way to work things out, in one shape or another.

We need to hold the big perspective to remind us that nature is one tough mother, and that life has so far survived the collision of continents, mountain ranges

---

* When the revolution comes, I am angling for a space on the ambiance committee.

erupting in volcanoes, murderously cold ice ages, the plague, Attila the Hun, and even Henry Kissinger. So there is reason for optimism. I took heart the other day when a friend who is an expert on Hindu prophecy told me that there are only 470,000 years left in the Kali Yuga, the era of destruction. Whew! We've turned the corner!

The big perspective also carries your intuitive understanding that you are part of it all, and so are *they*, the people whom the Dalai Lama calls "my friends, the enemy." Ours is a species-wide problem, and we're all in this survival game together. Besides, if your big picture does not talk about the bigger love then it won't transform anything.

My favorite big perspective is the epic of evolution, which offers us all forgiveness by revealing that we are a baby species, just getting started on our history. There were a hundred million generations of dinosaurs, at least ten million generations of mammals before humans came along, but there have only been twenty or thirty thousand generations of modern *Homo sapiens*. We only recently acquired these big brains and still don't know how to use them very well. Humans should not be tried as adults.

The story of evolution is also a good place to discover *self*-liberation. Contemporary biology tells us that we are all cells in a single living organism that is life on earth: the Greeks called that being Gaia, the goddess. Your life is not about *you* so much as it is about life itself, and when we feel ourselves to be part of this grand three-and-a-half-billion-year-old experiment, we can find meaning and purpose in working for its preservation.

If we look at ourselves in evolutionary history we also find hope, as we realize we are just now waking up to a radically different understanding of ourselves in the scheme of things. Lao Tzu, Socrates, and the Buddha appeared only 2,500 years ago—a blink of an eye in biological time—while Darwin, Freud, Jung, Einstein, and Hubble are virtually our contemporaries. We seem to be arriving at a whole new kind of consciousness. Of course we are feeling the growing pains as we move through this transition period, but maybe we will soon find a way to adapt to our latest story about human life.

Maybe we will even discover how to use our hearts and minds better, and finally learn how to be happy, or just learn how to be, which may be one and the same thing.

Along with your big perspective, I suggest that you also cultivate a hearty sense of humor and always keep it handy. As Wavy Gravy says, "If you don't have a sense of humor, it's just not funny." Remember that nobody really knows what's going on here, that we are all at the mercy of the great mystery. So admit your basic foolishness, laugh as much as possible, and step lightly through this world. You will cause less damage that way.

In the end, one of the most important things you can do is to love life, in all its fragile, bittersweet, fleeting beauty. The more you love it, the more energy you will find to help it heal.

2

That Old-time Religion

"All great truths begin as blasphemies."
GEORGE BERNARD SHAW

Humanity is now suffering through a deep spiritual crisis, and I assume that a major part of the problem lies with our gods and goddesses. After all, if they created everything, then whatever goes wrong is their fault.

I know that "god" is a delicate topic of inquiry, and some people feel very protective of their deity, so as I explore this subject I hope not to insult any true believers. I don't want to become the target of a fatwah or, god forbid, a crusade. I do not want men in iron suits chasing after me.

Let me be clear. I don't think it is wrong or even stupid to believe in god. In fact, I love the gods and goddesses, every single one of them. (If you love them all, then you're covered for sure.)

And how can you not love the gods? Sure, they started a lot of wars, sometimes got jealous and "smiteful," and, of course, they gave us politicians. On the other hand, just imagine all of the solace and wonder that deities have brought to humans over the course of our history—a feeling of being loved, special, blessed, saved. Think of all of those suffering people who wandered the desert, homeless and hungry, but kept on going because they believed they were god's "chosen people" on their way to a "promised land"; or the early Christians who walked out to face certain death in a lion's jaws but knew that they were eternally saved by Jesus's martyrdom; or the simple Hindu peasant who knows in her heart that the goddess Kali will bless her, if not in this life then the next; or the Sioux buffalo hunter who paid respects to the "great spirit" because that ritual would bring him meat to last the winter.

The only real problem with the gods is some of the humans who believe in them. Displaying a combination of ignorance and arrogance, people keep killing each other in the name of some particular god, or warring over the holy places where a god supposedly walked around or spoke to some prophets. These so-called *holy* wars have taken place throughout human history, but now we know that there have been hundreds of religions, featuring countless gods and goddesses, and that these deities change over time, and that no one tribe or people has a permanent lock on the one true god, and especially not on god's one true name.

Just think, the descendants of a family living near the Mediterranean through the last five millennia might have gone from believing, successively, in Chronos, Zeus, Jupiter, Jehovah, then adding Jesus. As with nation-states, even among the gods there is occasional regime change.

Indeed, the relativity of the gods was noticed way back in the fifth century B.C. by the historian Xenophanes, who wrote, "The Ethiopians say that their gods are snub-nosed and black, the Thracians that theirs have light blue eyes and red hair." And your god, what does he/she/it look like?

Most of us don't choose a god. It has been confirmed by surveys and research that your family, ethnic group, and geographical region will most likely determine which god you will worship. If you are Italian you were probably raised to believe in Jesus, and if you are Japanese you are likely to have Buddha or Jizo in your life. If you happen to have been born in a certain region of southwest Africa, you most likely were brought up to believe in the sky-god of the Herero people. That god's name is Ndjambi, whose name can only be spoken or written on special occasions. (Hopefully this was one of them.)

A lot of people still say they know for sure who god is, and if you don't believe in their particular god they can promise that when you die you will be placed in a burning hot cave where nasty, horned creatures will stick pitchforks into you and make you scream in pain, for ever and ever. Isn't it time we got over that vengeful, adolescent horror of a mythology?! Sometimes I can only pray: "May God save us from the people who believe in Him."

Why should we care if people use a different name for god than we do? I can't imagine any respectable deity saying with menace, "Hey buddy, what did you call me?" So why should you be bothered if someone calls god "Omega" or "Yoohoo" or "Martha Reeves and the Vandellas?" I can imagine that someday the heavens will part, and we will all hear a booming voice saying, "Humans! You all got my name wrong! [pause] And I forgive you." There is a chance that god doesn't even have a name. There's even a good chance that god isn't a *being*, or at least not some humanlike being. Do you think we are so good-looking that a god—who could look like anything or nothing—would actually want to look like us? "Vanity of vanity," sayeth the Preacher.

And yet, I would guess that most of you reading this will have a certain picture of god, and lo and behold, He's an Italian! He's got a long flowing white beard and long hair, and looks somewhat like an aging bohemian. I'm referring, of course, to the god who lives up there on the ceiling of the Sistine Chapel, that buffed, handsome older dude with the life-giving finger.

If you'll remember, the Jews said we were not supposed to make a graven image of God, which seems like a real advance in humanity's god-ideas. It also allowed the Jews to save a lot of money on statues.

✱ ✱ ✱ ✱ ✱

Meanwhile, I have a modest suggestion for how we can deal with humanity's god problems. First of all, we call all the gods together for a "summit meeting." Maybe this meeting could be held on Mt. Olympus, or somewhere in the Himalayas, where there are already a lot of gods around who could host the gathering. (There will have to be separate tables: Bacchus needs wine, whereas Buddha won't touch the stuff; Demeter wants corn for dinner, Jehovah likes lamb; Zoroaster wants candles for a centerpiece, while Tor would like an ice sculpture.)

Once we got all the gods together, we would beseech them—all of us beseeching our own particular deity—to do humanity a great big favor and decide on a common name. Since I'm the only one working on this project, I will take the liberty to propose this new name.

First of all, if you'll notice, many of the names we already use for deities end in the syllable "ah." Jehov*ah;* All*ah;* Brahm*a;* Tar*a;* Dian*a;* Krishn*a.* So maybe we could get the gods to accept the common nickname "Ah."

It's a perfect name. "Ah" is the first sound that most of us make when we are born, "w ... aaaah!" and the last sound we make as we die, exhaling, "Ah ..." So the first moments of our life would automatically become a prayer, and the last moment's "Ah" would be a sigh, signaling our complete release from this hard duty as a human. I suppose people could still use their special tribal names for god, but emphasize the last vowel, "ah" and we would all agree that we are talking about the same ultimate, almighty. Ah! The one who is totally ah-some!

Another possibility is to give our highest deity the name "Ma," which is the same word in many human languages, referring to mother. Then, instead of looking up as we pray, toward "our father who art in heaven," we would look down at the earth, the womb of all life, the goddess who the Greeks called Gaia. (There's another "ah," for you.)

Maybe we could even use both names, Ah and Ma. We could divide god into two, a male and female, yin and yang, just as it was for a few clever humans in our ancient history. "Ah Ma! Ma Ah! Ah-ha Ma!" The possibilities for songs and praises are endless.

The First Church of Scientific Science

"DEFINITION: God is the shortest distance between zero and infinity. In which direction? one may ask. We shall reply that His first name is not Jack, but Plus-and-Minus. And one should say: ±God is the shortest distance between 0 and infinity, in either direction."

ALFRED JARRY, DADAIST PHILOSOPHER

For many of us in the modern world, science has replaced religion as the purveyor of truth. But we have yet to develop any new symbols or rituals that will place modern science into a spiritual or religious context. We should consider creating "The First Church of Scientific Science." Let's go inside. . . .

Saint Isaac and Albert's Cathedral. The ceiling is a large circular planetarium, which revolves with the earth and displays an accurate view of the heavens to the very limit of astronomical exploration. With computer graphics, the scene on the ceiling is expanding at the same rate as the universe itself.

In the naves of the cathedral are holograms of the Saints of Science, each of them at the moment of their revelation: Heraclitus standing in his ever-changing river; Galileo looking through his telescope at the stars; Euclid with his ruler and triangle; Newton with a ripe apple on his head; Einstein at the blackboard with his chalk and pipe; Schrödinger with his cat on his shoulder; Heisenberg looking uncertain.

The stained-glass windows around the chapel show us scenes from the story of evolution. Present-day Homo sapiens sapiens *is pictured first as you enter the church, so that as you approach the altar you are moving backward in time.*

Just before you reach the altar, the second-to-the-last of the windows shows a one-celled organism, and the last window is filled with a double-helix strand of DNA.

On stage at the back of the church, on either side of the altar, sit two giant statues—replicas of a hydrogen and a helium atom. All across the back wall of the church, electrified models of other atoms (enlarged of course) are spinning in their orbits, crashing into each other, exploding into flashes of light, and giving churchgoers a sense of the ever-changing dynamic reality of charged particles.

In the center, where the Crucifix or Ark of the Torah normally stands, is the sacred symbol of the First Church of Science. It is an emblem of six white dots on a field of black—a representation of the six known quarks! The ground of being. The Holy Sextet: Up, Down, Top, Bottom, Strange, and Charmed. AMEN. The black field represents the emptiness from which it all sprang, or the black hole from which it all emerged, or perhaps the "dark area," the last mystery still to be solved—the first cause.

We enter the church during prayers—the congregation, all dressed in white lab coats is reciting the liturgy—the table of basic elements. "Hydrogen. Helium. Lithium.

Berylium. Boron. Carbon." Special emphasis is given to the last syllable of each word, making the cathedral resonate with "ums" and "ons." *Soon the supplicants will bow their heads and pray that somebody will come up with a Unified Field Theory. Finally, the congregation will chant the Church of Science's great Mantra, a mantra that not only contains the seed syllables of the universe but also is the name of the seed itself. The sacred mantra . . . ATOM AH HUM, ATOM AH HUM, ATOM AH HUM.*

3

"Once Upon a Spacetime . . ."

"That the world is, is the mystical."
LUDWIG WITTGENSTEIN

We have a new creation myth being told by our species, a new story about the origins and workings of the universe. It is the story of the evolution of the cosmos, and therefore a new story about you and me; if there are beings on another planet in a different galaxy, it is their story too. This is Universal Pictures.

We'll begin our new story at the very beginning, and

even though this is the "scientific" story of the universe we can at least start with the first words of the Bible: "In the beginning . . ." And since this is a creation myth, we should try to put in some appropriate flourishes: "In the beginning, *sayeth the scientists, . . . there was nothing.* And it was good."

We can at least presume it was good. Nothing could ever be wrong with nothing.

According to the scientists, in the beginning there wasn't even any space, so there was no place to put anything. In the beginning, they say, there wasn't any time, so nothing ever got done, and nobody cared. Therefore, let it be said once again, "It was good."

And so it came to pass, that 13.7 billion years ago *today* (we can't be sure about today being the actual anniversary of the birth of the universe, but it certainly could have been) there occurred an auspicious event called "THE BIG BANG."

But if nothing existed, then what banged? A few people raised this question, and a little while later some scientists decided that there must have been something after all. They called it a "singularity," which they describe as "particle-like" and smaller than an atom but infinitely dense.*

Whether there was nothing at all or a tiny, infinitely dense singularity is not known for sure, but almost all scientists will agree that the universe began with this explosion of whatever was or wasn't there. This "Big Bang" story of creation doesn't say who or what caused the initial explosion, or why it needed to happen. So the *bigger* mysteries remain. Scientists can, however, report that this universe we inhabit and are made out of started off with that bang, the first thing that ever happened.

The first things created by the Big Bang were space and time, which are necessary if you're going to have everything else. You aren't going to make a piece of furniture unless there's someplace to put it, and you'll need time to put it to use. By the way, we now know that space and time are not separate, but happen only in conjunction with each other as space-time. So let's eliminate the hyphen and start getting comfortable

---

* Remember, when scientists say "infinitely" they really mean it.

with them as a single quality. Spacetime. (Lightdark. Updown. Youandeverythingelse.)

And so it came to pass that streaming out of the Big Bang came enough spacetime for an entire universe to evolve into, and following that came the elementary forces and elementary particles and eventually the elementary elements, and they began mixing and morphing and proliferating, eventually creating billions of galaxies, full of billions of suns and planets, along with the earth and all its mountains and oceans and forests and fish and people and birds and bugs and buildings and cars and bicycles and pizza and shoes and socks and you and me and everything else we can know of and name. And it all came out of the explosion of a tiny dot much smaller than an atom.

Sure, Mr. Scientist. Whatever you say. Your story is at least as plausible as the one about the god who creates everything in six days. And besides, you're talking science here.

For a better picture of the birth of our universe, consider that a trillionth of a trillionth of a trillionth of a second after the Big Bang, the universe was about three feet in diameter. The entire universe was once the size of a large beach ball! Now that's a universe you can get your mind around. However, just one *minute* after the Big Bang, the universe was a million billion miles in diameter. That was a very, very, very big bang, causing the universe to grow with unimaginable speed, every nanosecond adding huge new reaches of spacetime to its size.

One astrophysicist estimates that the universe is now about ten billion trillion trillion cubic light years large. Does that sound right to you? Ten billion trillion trillion cubic light years? Okay, *approximately*.

Remember, we are talking about *your* birth, here. The astrophysicists' creation story is not just about a universe that you inhabit, it is about *you*: a recounting of the stream of events that you bubbled out of; about the primal flash of light that is still visible in your eyes; about the weightless and dimensionless particles that turned into a gas that turned into the earth that then turned into your flesh.

And the Big Bang keeps big banging away, inside of each of us. Our living energy is the heat and light generated by the primal flash. Every time you move your hand or take a step you are expressing the energy of the Big Bang. And right now, inside your head, millions of synapses are firing. At least we hope so. That is the energy of the Big Bang trying to comprehend the Big Bang. We are pieces of the universe, wondering about itself.

Our new creation story is about everything else as well—the chair, the lamp, the paper, the floor, the air. As I look around me and try to imagine it all emerging out of that primal ball of heat and energy, I am puzzled. How did the original fireball get itself into all these different shapes, each seeming to have some purpose or function? What a magical display has been created by that single explosion! I find that having some description of the beginning of this universe, as impossible as it is to imagine, provides me with a sense of the mystery and majesty of all things. I also see that I am part of a much bigger project than this Wes Nisker drama. I see that I am one with it all. Everything was born with me, on my birthday, and we are all growing old together.

❊ ❊ ❊ ❊ ❊

"Things are not as they seem. Nor are they otherwise."
ZEN SAYING

It turns out that this universe we live in is a real trickster. For instance, it may appear that there's a lot of stuff here—mountains and oceans and clusters of galaxies and the like—but there's really not much stuff here at all. Because everything we can perceive is made of atoms, and atoms are 99 percent empty space. Inside the atom, the tiny particles circling the nucleus are proportionally miles away. There's hardly any matter to matter!

So, consider this: if your body is made out of atoms and atoms are 99 percent empty space, what is holding your clothes on? Not only does the emperor have no clothes, the clothes hardly have any emperor.

We see the world on a relatively gross level, as if it were composed of solid, identifiable objects. But in fact, it's an optical illusion. As it says in the Buddhist Heart Sutra, "Form is emptiness, and emptiness is form."

Of course the scientists have broken the atom down

further, into three basic subatomic particles—quarks, leptons, and gluons*—and some physicists say that everything in the universe is made out of them, that is, at the most basic level of matter, these three particles are all that exist. So why does it look like there are so many different things? If my hand is made of the same stuff as the chair and the grass, how does that stuff know how to get itself into all the different shapes and textures?

Even more puzzling is the discovery of *anti-matter*. The scientists say the universe is full of anti-matter, and that every time a particle of matter meets a particle of anti-matter the two annihilate each other. If you believe in a god, the existence of anti-matter might indicate that your god was somewhat ambivalent about creating the universe in the first place. Your creator would get it started with a batch of matter, have second thoughts ("What a lot of trouble it will be!"), and then produce a batch of anti-matter. And so on.

The discovery of anti-matter does raise some impor-

---

* I don't know exactly how it works, but I think the gluons are there to hold the quarks and leptons together. At least that's how it sounds. "Glue-ons."

tant new questions for humans. Now we not only have to ask "What's the matter?" but also "What's the *anti-matter?*" Of course, the answers will always contradict each other. Leading to the deeper question: "Does it matter?"

Scientists are trying to answer all remaining questions with the "Theory of Everything," the latest version being the "Superstring Theory," which says that everything in the universe is nothing but minuscule, vibrating strings of energy. (To tell one thing from another, just "check out the vibes." We knew a few things back in the '60s.) The superstrings are so small, according to the physicists, that the size of one string is to the size of a human being as the size of a human being is to the universe. We don't have a word for that degree of smallness. So, of course, nobody has ever seen a superstring, but the physicists and mathematicians say they have figured it all out and that the strings do exist, vibrating along underneath all our realities.

Superstring Theory also says there are seven more dimensions to reality, dimensions that somehow didn't unfold in our universe and thus remain hidden. I think that's probably a good thing, because we can barely manage the four dimensions we now live in—height, width, depth, and time. If there were seven more dimensions to reality, imagine how much harder it would be to find your car keys or keep your weight down. Maybe one of those hidden dimensions is where birds go to die. Maybe one dimension is full of lost socks.

Even if there are seven more dimensions, physicists now suspect what the mystics have been saying for eons, which is that reality itself is just a trick of our mind. The most widely accepted interpretation of quantum physics, the "Copenhagen Interpretation," says, and I quote, "There is no reality in the absence of observation." As one physicist put it, "Only when we are looking are there particles. When we aren't looking, there are only waves . . . *probability* waves."

This interpretation of quantum physics is also known as "the wave particle duality" and is part of the principle known as "uncertainty," which basically says we don't know what the hell is going on here.

It does sound absurd to imagine that when nobody is looking at, say, the ceiling in your room, it doesn't exist. It still keeps out the rain and the sun. Einstein said, "I can't believe that the moon disappears when nobody is looking."

Maybe there is some kind of cosmic consciousness that is always looking at everything. One story claims that some Tibetan monks are sitting in a cave in the Himalayas, holding the world together by just paying attention. They know that we all have to live through the karma of life in this earthly realm.

I imagine a Zen monk saying, "No mind, no matter. No matter, never mind."

The conclusion that the physicists are coming to, contrary to everything our senses tell us, is that there is no-*thing* in this universe. Remember, at the very core of matter they found energy. "$E = mc^2$." Everything is vibrating, in a constant state of flux, change, movement.

One physicist claims, "Matter is just gravitationally trapped light." The universe is a light show. If we could look through electron microscope glasses we would just see flowing streams of energy, if anything. Our current sensate picture slows down the flow, but there is still nothing solid or lasting. In reality, there is no-*thing*-ness.

I find it very funny, and perhaps the penultimate irony, that in a civilization like ours, so thoroughly devoted to materialism, our esteemed scientists have discovered that matter doesn't really exist! We are optical illusions, chasing our own tails and traces.

As Samuel Beckett wrote, "Nothing is more real than nothing." And as the Buddha said, "Thus shall ye view this world: like a star at dawn, a bubble in a stream, a flash of lightning in a summer cloud, a flickering lamp, a phantom, or a dream."

4

Please Identify Yourself

"The true value of a human being is determined primarily by the measure and the sense in which he has attained liberation from the self."

ALBERT EINSTEIN

When I heard someone on the radio explaining the new crime of "identity theft," I immediately thought, "Yes! Rob *me*, please! Take my identity, and leave the cash!"

During my lifelong practice of Buddhist meditation I have lost several identities. In fact, I was drawn to the practice because I was trying to run away from myself—the sentimental, histrionic drama of me-ness. The Buddha says that the false conceit of "I" or "self" is the bane of our existence, and I was indeed relieved when I began to see through the various membranes of personal identity. But what really surprised and delighted me is what I saw on the other side. It turns out I am not who I thought I was—I'm much, much more than that.

For the most part, we each live in our own story, and it's pretty much the only one we tell, as though we have a scratch in our mental record, so that the same lines get repeated, over and over again—*my* finances, *my* friends, *my* family, *my* stuff.

It's too bad, because while each of us is lost in our private drama, we don't notice that we are taking part in grand epics and heroic, noble projects. For instance, even while reading e-mail or shopping for socks, we continue to operate as cells in the great body of life on earth, part of a fascinating, multibillion year experiment in biology and consciousness. To recognize ourselves in that role can be a skillful means of self-liberation, and a deep source of pleasure.

Of course, in your own story you are always the star, but in the big story of life on earth, you are just a bit player. In fact, an itty-bitty bit player, just a momentary walk-on part. But that is the point. "You" can disappear into this grand perspective, like walking into a Chinese landscape painting and getting swallowed up by the deep gorges of bamboo forest and eternal sky. You can move out of the personal into increasingly large circles of inclusion and identity until finally you can point in any direction and say, along with the great Indian mystics, "Tat tvam asi," "I am that."

Whenever I ask people to identify themselves, most will come up with information about their gender, nationality, religion, career, marital and parental status, sometimes even personality ("I'm a happy fellow." "I'm moody." "I'm a type 'A'."). When pressed to define themselves further, some will remember their identity as a mammal. But so far, hardly anyone has thought to answer, "I'm an earthling." And not one person has claimed as part of their identity the phylum to which they belong. Come on, say it with me and say it loud—"I'm a vertebrate, and I'm proud!"

If you picture yourself inside of epic stories such as evolution, you can find relief from your personal drama. You access what some eco-philosophers and modern mystics call "deep time," where you experience yourself subsumed in history, biology, geology, and even physics. All personal outlines fade into these big pictures.

The Buddha explained the effect to his son Rahula, noting that if you take a teaspoon of salt and place it in a glass of water, it will make the water taste salty. But if you put the same teaspoon of salt in the Ganges river, it won't affect the water's taste. Likewise, your personal drama will dissolve in the seven seas of history and the great ocean of spacetime.

Thirteenth-century Zen master Eihei Dogen was one who loved to inhabit the big stories. He throws us lines such as, "The entire universe is the true human body."

Dogen's teachings often point to the issue of identity,

and he sums up the Buddha's teaching this way: "To study Buddhism is to study the self; to study the self is to know the self; to know the self is to forget the self; and to forget the self is to become one with all the myriad things of the world."

That's what started happening in my meditation practice. As I became less identified with my personal drama, I became more acquainted with my "species self," which in turn led me to feel connected to all other living beings.

In fact, one of the best things I ever learned from meditation is that I'm alive. While this should be obvious to all of us, I had never let this truth reverberate inside me, or become part of my identity. Over time, the sensations of my body and breath have come to carry the mark of all life. I think of the poet Kabir, who instructs us to feel "the breath inside the breath," pointing to the grand mystery that pulses inside each of us and is common to all. Now I know of myself as one of the living! I am a *live* one!

You too are a member of the *sangha,* the community, of the living. Welcome. Glad you could make it. Life on earth is now appearing as "_____" (your name here).

Occasionally, I will feel my breath and reflect on the calculation that in an average life we get about thirteen million breaths. I sometimes wonder which millionth I'm on now.

The path of meditation can lead through a playground of shifting identity. One of my meditation teachers, S. N. Goenka, told me to sweep my body with awareness, and slowly but surely I became familiar with my nose and my toes, and what poet Mary Oliver calls the world of "lime and appetite, the oceanic fluids." This bag of bones and seawater came alive and started to take over from my ego as the foundation of my identity. You might say I was "born again" as elements of nature; and again, as an animal. I had joined a grand and venerable *sangha*.

The dharma path kept me shape-shifting until eventually I came to a shapeless shape, the ocean of consciousness, the "empty," "shining," "radiant," "magic," "luminous" awareness, as the Tibetans are wont to exclaim. And although it is often blissful in that pure awareness realm, "I" also get bored with it. I mean, how much radiant emptiness can you stand? That's when I take refuge and delight in my relative identity as part of the living mass of this planet. I just think of the aliveness as an intermediate step on the path to the deathless. And as Thoreau says, "Shall I not have intelligence with the earth? Am I not partly leaves and vegetable mould myself?"

When I place myself in the story of evolution, I also feel a surge of compassion for the struggles of all life. Let's face it, the basic rules on this planet are a bitch. But the Buddhist blessing "May all beings be happy" has a deeper ring to it when I regard myself in the same world as those who dress in feathers, fur, scales, leaves, and bark.

Seeing myself in the light of biological history is very forgiving. When I find myself full of fear or desire, I remember that I am dealing with a brain and nervous system that has been hard-wired for millions of years for these emotions. Then I apply one of my favorite mantras, "I'm perfectly human." When I sit in meditation as a human being rather than as an individual, I feel I am part of a collective effort on the part of our species to right itself, to find a new sanity. As Robert Thurman says of meditation, "It's evolutionary sport." In the light of that big perspective, I thank you for being on my team.

5

I Hadn't Thought of That

"Just as we can walk without thinking, we can also think without thinking."

MARVIN MINSKY, COGNITIVE SCIENTIST

After years of meditation practice, one of the most significant changes in my life has been in my relationship to my mind. We're still living together, of course, and we remain friends. But my mind and I are no longer codependent. I am slowly but surely gaining my freedom.

The change in our relationship started when I finally

acknowledged that my mind had a thinking problem. It was a heavy thinker, often starting with two or three thoughts the minute I got up in the morning and then continuing to think throughout the day until bedtime when it would need a couple of thoughts in order to fall asleep.

My mind produced thought after thought, about love and work, along with existential thoughts and trashy ones, thoughts about clothing, food, music, politics—one subject after another, on and on, and all of it centered around me, of course, which became embarrassing, as well as oppressive. All the thinking would not let me "be"—either at ease, without worry, or in the moment. I began to see my mind as an insecure, selfish, nagging bitch who was stealing my happiness and destroying my life. For our mutual survival, I decided to seek an intervention.

At first I tried analysis, with hopes of uncovering the psychological origin of my mind's need to think; later I got into some gestalt screaming, flailing, and crying, which only temporarily stopped the flow of thinking; and intermittently I used drugs, trying to "blow my mind" by short-circuiting the neural wiring. Finally, I found meditation.

I soon discovered that the goal of meditation was not to stop thinking, as I had assumed, but rather to expose my mind to itself. Before meditation I was completely focused on the content of thoughts, how to manipulate them and extract meaning from them. That is what I was graded on in school and what our culture considers important. But nobody had taught me how to look at the process of thinking itself or at the intrinsic nature of thought. As the Tibetan sage Tulku Urgen said, "The stream of thoughts surges through the mind of an ordinary person, who will have no knowledge whatsoever about who is thinking, where the thought comes from, and where the thought disappears. The person will be totally and mindlessly carried away by one thought after another!"

Let's be clear: thinking is not bad, or some kind of roadblock to enlightenment. In fact, thinking is an essential tool of our well-being and even our survival.*

---

* Perhaps a warning sign should be put up at meditation centers advising all who enter on the path: "You give up thinking at your own risk."

Indeed, thinking is fabulous. Our genius as a species is the ability to create complex symbols, agree on their meaning, and use them to encode our knowledge and describe our plans. The thinking function allows us to compute, reason, and imagine, and perhaps most important of all, to share our understanding with each other in the form of speech or writing. We can even record our thinking and pass it on to future generations. ("Hold that thought!")

Unfortunately, as a species we have grown to value thinking to the exclusion of other aspects of our being. The more we become identified with our thoughts, the more we are lost in our individual narrative, disconnected from what we have in common with other humans and other forms of life. We have turned our sense of self over to our thinking mind, leaving us "lost" in thought, disembodied. Especially in our culture, heads are us.

Although we remain convinced that our ability to think somehow makes us "the chosen species," existentially superior to rest of creation, in the modern era this belief is being challenged. In his secret notebooks, Charles Darwin wondered, "Why is thought—which is a secretion of the brain—deemed to be so much more wonderful than, say, gravity, which is a property of matter? It is only our arrogance, our admiration of ourselves." Making the same point, Stephen Jay Gould wondered if an intelligent octopus would go around being so proud of its eight arms.

Meanwhile, the new cognitive sciences are revealing that our thoughts are not the dominant player in our lives, not leading in the dance. Research into our brain and nervous system finds that most of our interpretation of the world as well as our decision making takes place on what Daniel Dennett calls the "subpersonal" level, without a rational, conscious, thinking self directing or guiding the process. In fact, brain science reveals that thinking arises quite late in the cognitive sequence, in order to weave our experience into the ongoing story we tell about ourselves. As science fiction writer Robert Heinlein once noted, "Man is not a rational animal, but a rationalizing one." Our thinking is, for the most part, an afterthought.

Do we overvalue our thinking? The scientists seem to "think" so. Those who study cognition say it is a way of organizing experience, while the evolutionary scientists see it as an adaptation, something that evolved like the eye or the opposable thumb. A great tool, folks, but not the be-all and end-all of creation.

The Buddha would appear to agree with Darwin and the scientists. He regarded the mind as a sixth sense and did not seem to give thinking any more or less importance than sight or hearing. Like the other five senses, our thinking is simply another way of reading and interpreting the world. And like the other senses, the main job of the thinking mind is survival.

Just try to imagine what humans were thinking twenty thousand years ago. I would guess it was something along the lines of "I wonder who is going on the hunt tomorrow?" or "The gods want me to put red clay on my face to make the enemy run away" or "Honey, who is watching the fire tonight?" Today our thoughts are about our medical insurance, or the news from around the world, or our love life (aka passing on our genes), but the story remains the same. Playing on most of our interior human screens throughout history is an episode of *Survivor*.

When I regard thinking as essentially a survival tool, it helps me to see my thoughts as generic, as endemic to my species, not as "I," "me," or "mine."

After years of meditation, and with the help of modern science, I no longer have to believe in or get carried away by every thought that comes along. Now I can turn to the thinking part of my mind and say, "Sorry, I'm not going to think about that right now. I'm busy." I haven't learned how to stop my thoughts, but I have learned how to ignore them.

That leaves me with only one problem: Now that I've gained some independence from the flow of thoughts, sometimes I don't know what to think. Still, it's a small price to pay.

6

Much Ado About Nothing

"To see the truth, contemplate all phenomena as a lie."
THAGANAPA, TIBETAN SAGE

In recent years I have been studying a Tibetan Buddhist teaching called *dzogchen*, meaning "the natural
great perfection." The goal of dzogchen is to become
intimate with "mind" as the source of all reality; to
experience consciousness as the ground of being. I
heard about dzogchen while traveling in India in the
early '70s and was told that it was nearly impossible to

receive transmission of this ultimate in esoteric wisdom without many years of arduous preliminary practices. Finally, in the '90s, some Tibetan masters began teaching dzogchen in the United States, and I was able to sign up for a retreat with a young Tibetan teacher named Tsoknyi Rinpoche.

In one of his first instructions, Tsoknyi told us, "Look in between your thoughts, because in the gap between thoughts is where you will see the pure, empty nature of mind, the ultimate truth of who you are."

"How strange," I thought to myself. I had always assumed, along with my entire civilization, that the ultimate truth would come to me in the form of thoughts, not in between them. We are used to having our truths expressed in meaningful sentences, and I figured that the *ultimate* truth would come, maybe in big, block letters, or flashing on and off, "THIS IS WHAT IT'S ALL ABOUT . . ." and then the answer would follow. But now these Tibetans were telling me that my thoughts were obscuring the truth.

As I began to study dzogchen, I remembered that

throughout my life I had been looking for ways to "blow my mind." Along with many of my generation, I had sought relief from the analyzing, judging, segregating, self-conscious, thinking mind. Perhaps I intuitively knew all along that the ultimate truth was lying somewhere in the cracks.

Although it may sound ridiculous, a few days into the dzogchen retreat we were told that the empty essence of mind can be glimpsed more easily in the moments immediately after sneezing or having an orgasm. The dzogchen masters are quite serious about these opportunities to see the truth.*

I was especially fascinated by one technique where the teacher yells, "Phet!" or suddenly slams his hand down on a podium or strikes a bell, and at the sound the student is instructed to quickly "look at what is looking." It's a funny game of trying to sneak up on yourself, to slip past your ego, which of course knows what you are up to and is ready to take evasive maneuvers to

---

* Since we had taken vows of celibacy, at least for the duration of the retreat, and because I didn't have any pepper or other sneeze inducer handy, this information did me absolutely no good at the time.

prevent you from seeing through all your thoughts and the illusion of self—into the bare essence of mind.

And what precisely did I see in those moments when I saw into the gap between thoughts? Well, first of all there wasn't any *me* there. Knowing was there (sometimes referred to as "Knowledge-Awareness") and a brief moment of knowing that knowing was there (knowing was knowing the knowing), but "I" was not involved. In fact, there wasn't even any *there* there. The knowing had no location and seemed like some kind of elemental force field, an omnipresent quality of the universe itself.

One dzogchen text, *The Flight of the Garuda*, puts it in appropriate devotional language: "The primal awareness of self-existing Knowledge manifests every-thing. . . . It is unchanging and unchangeable. . . . It is the pure-being of Immutable Diamond. . . . It is the pure being of Boundless Light-form." In dzogchen, the power of knowing is spoken of in reverent tones, perhaps because "mind" is considered the one universal source, almost as if it were a deity.

* * * * *

I don't know when I first realized it, but for as long as I can remember I have known that all things are one. In the '60s, the counterculture expressed this idea with the phrase "everything is everything." That saying was always a conversation stopper, because once it is spoken no further distinctions can be made. But the phrase reflected a growing awareness among my generation that all of reality is a single, interwoven process. The mystics had been telling us this for centuries, and the physicists have recently confirmed it. (They say all of reality is *entangled*.) Now dzogchen was offering me the *experience* of the "oneness."

When I first began my spiritual journey, I was convinced that if I could merge with the oneness then my painful self-consciousness would be stripped away, nirvana would kick in, and the bliss would begin. I understand now that trying to become one with the oneness is like playing musical chairs with yourself. You are already "in" the oneness. However, in spite of the fact that there's nowhere to get to, you've still got to make some effort or you won't remember that you are already there. Another problem is that when you do realize you are there, then "you" aren't there. Nobody is around to enjoy the experience. Oneness and you-ness don't go together. So what's the point of getting there?

Most mystics agree that ultimate reality is virtually indescribable, but they've given it many names: the Tao, the Source, the "is-ness," the unborn. I've even heard it pronounced "the unnameable," a name that seems to cancel itself out. Jack Kerouac wrote, "I call it the golden eternity but you can call it anything you want." I like the Zen term "suchness," which has a funky, down-home ring to it. "I'm just going out on the porch for a spell, folks, and sit around in the good ol' suchness."

The Tibetan dzogchen masters have come up with a lot of great names for their ultimate reality, often expressed in the spontaneous *dohas*, poems of amazement and appreciation for the "natural great perfection." Their names include: "the predicateless, primordial essence"; "the weaver of the web of appearances"; "the transcendent fullness of the emptiness" (have yourself a waltz with that paradox!); "the dissolver of space, time, and *sangsaric* mind"; and "the outbreather and inbreather of infinite universes throughout the endlessness of duration."

But what's in a name? What I wanted was the *experience* of oneness, and in the dzogchen retreat I felt that I was almost home.

In spite of the tricky dzogchen mind games, at one point the teacher emphasized that we did not have to struggle to find the natural great perfection. In fact, a major part of the dzogchen practice (sometimes called *non*-meditation) seemed to consist of just relaxing the mind. We were told not to do anything or try to construct any particular mental state or conditions, but to just let the mind be open and natural, without a central focus. I found that this simple instruction led quite often to an experience of a grand perspective into which the sense of self was totally subsumed. "I" disappeared into the universal mind. As it says in the Tibetan dzogchen text *Flight of the Garuda*: "Searching for the meditator, if you fail to find him, then your meditation is at the point of resolution."

Okay. That's easy—if you are other than a living

being on Planet Earth. It is the nature of life to central-
ize into oneself. Birds do it, bees do it, and even *unedu-
cated* fleas do it! The very definition of life, according
to the new biology, includes the process of "autopoe-
sis," or *self*-creating. We humans have developed a very
solid and vivid sense of individuality, but we can also
see through the boundaries and understand ourselves in
context. That's why the Buddha called this the *precious*
human existence. Once you see that nobody is seeing,
and that "knowing" is what is knowing, and that the
mind creating your reality is actually the *Mind* with a
capital "M," then your sense of separateness begins to
disappear. You have finally come home. Then, as Woody
Allen says, "Those achieving oneness can now move on
to twoness."

✻ ✻ ✻ ✻ ✻

Like the dzogchen masters, Western science has also
found "knowing" to be one of the central mysteries of
existence. The neuroscientists call it "the hard problem"
of consciousness. They have been looking around inside

the brain, but can't seem to figure out what exactly this knowing consists of, where it is located, or how it is produced. Francisco Varela, a student of Tibetan Buddhism and a renowned biologist, claimed that "knowing" is the very quality that defines life, and that "to live is to know." Every living being, including the single-celled organism, "knows," at least enough to receive and react to information in the environment. If life is synonymous with knowing, then a bow to one is a bow to the other.

I haven't "believed" in anything for a long time, but dzogchen practice has turned me toward awareness as something worthy of reverence. I haven't exactly seen god in the gaps, but I find that knowing now represents the whole mystery of existence for me. It arouses my curiosity and sense of wonder—about all that lives and all that knows.

7

Come On, Get Happy

"My opinion is that you will never find happiness until you stop looking for it."

TAOIST MASTER CHUANG TZU

"Happiness is a fatality," wrote the poet Rimbaud. I remember being somewhat puzzled when I first read that line, and then feeling a sense of ease and liberation wash over me. Turning the idea of happiness on its head had suddenly made me very happy.

I would guess that happiness has ruined many a life since it was invented, which may not have been so long ago. It is doubtful that our prehistoric human ancestors had any idea of "happiness," distinct from what it felt like to satisfy basic needs. If the wolf was not at the door and there was enough food around for a few days, your ordinary Mr. or Ms. Homo habilis was probably quite happy, even by our standards. He or she just didn't know it. Being happy wasn't an issue. It wasn't on anybody's to-do list.

Now, we all want happiness. The American Declaration of Independence even proclaims that all humans have the right to pursue it, which implies, of course, that happiness is out there somewhere and for some reason is running away.

Even though I know better now, I still catch myself believing that I can grab happiness and take it home with me. I keep uncovering, hidden beneath my plans and fantasies, the assumption that if I can just get a hold of whatever I feel is lacking in my life at the moment— an empty mind, enough money, a great house—then I will "become" happy. I might as well wish for a magic carpet, special potion, or power ring.

Maybe we aren't supposed to be happy. Scientists have done experiments on the standard mammalian brain and found that it is not built for happiness. It functions so that, as neurologist Melvin Konner explains, "the organism's chronic internal state will be a vague mixture of anxiety and desire—best described by the phrase 'I want,' spoken with or without an object for the verb." Surely you are familiar with that brain, having seen it up close and personal, always twitching with dissatisfaction, never at peace.

It could be that nature is simply not selecting for happiness in mammals because it isn't useful for survival. At those times when you are feeling happy you won't be on the alert for trouble and therefore your life will be in jeopardy. The anxious people turn out to be the lucky ones, likely to live a long life. Sure, it will be unhappy, but at least it will be long. Happy people are the ones who really have something to worry about.

My definition of happiness has changed over the years. When I was younger, I defined myself as happy when I was engaged in an activity that stimulated my nervous system and made my heart beat faster. We used to call that feeling "a rush." I was happy, therefore, at rock-and-roll concerts where the high decibel levels automatically caused my blood vessels to con-strict. Recently I had a rock-and-roll concert experi-ence, and the feeling was mainly one of irritation and discomfort.

I have often confused pleasure with happiness, especially when I was younger. Pleasant sensations can accompany happiness, but what we call pleasure is a particular experience of the senses and usually includes some kind of intensity. Pleasure is the feeling you get when you step into a shower or a hot bath, or when you first bite into something that tastes good. If you ask your-self, you may not be particularly happy at that moment, even though you are having pleasant sensations.*

Happiness may look different to people with cer-tain temperaments. The reclusive types will feel happier alone, while those with a gene for "novelty seeking" will be happiest when on a quest for a new experience.

---

* The act of sex is one of the most pleasurable experiences we can have, no doubt designed that way by evolution to keep us reproducing. When we have sex, many parts of our being—the nerve endings in our skin, the pleasure centers in the brain, the psyche, and maybe even our genes themselves—are all standing up and shouting, "Yes, go baby go, this is what you are alive to do!" But as many know, you can enjoy sex and still be sad.

Those who have a need to accomplish will feel happiest when busy with their work. As Albert Camus wrote about the ambitious ones, "The struggle toward the heights is enough to fill a man's heart. One must imagine Sisyphus happy."

People believe that they create their own happiness or sadness, but common sense tells us that is a false assumption. If you were truly in charge of your emotions, wouldn't you be happy all the time?

How do you even know when you are happy? What exactly does it feel like? That question is similar to the one asked by the cartoon character Zippy the Pinhead, "Are we having fun yet?" What does happiness feel like as a physical sensation? What is in your mind when you are happy? The better question may be to ask what is *not* in your mind.

These questions arose for me when I first began to meditate, which also started to alter my definition of happiness. Strange as it now seems to me, I was twenty-six years old before I first experienced the inner contentment that I now call happiness. Before meditation, I had never experienced such moments and therefore had no way to measure them against pleasure or other degrees of happiness. Oh sure, there had been some post-coital, post-meal, or post-work moments when I felt a kind of self-satisfaction, but that kind of happiness usually did not last very long. In meditation, for the first time I felt the happiness of being at ease; I was released from the compulsion of the most primal of instincts as well as from my personal likes and dislikes. My mind was at peace with itself and the world.

The Buddha taught that kind of happiness. He put it this way: "True happiness can only be found by eliminating the false idea of 'I' or 'self.'" Only then is the survival brain turned down and the personality fever cooled. The only problem with that formulation is that once the "I" or "self" has been eliminated, then there is no one around to enjoy the feeling of happiness. Damn, it's always something.

8

I Love Science

"Once I was a cloud. Once I was a rock. This is not poetry. This is science."

VIETNAMESE BUDDHIST MASTER THICH
NHAT HANH

As I was growing up I didn't like science very much. It seemed to me like a lot of empty facts, bits of knowledge about the formation of the planets or atomic valence—stuff that I had to memorize but didn't matter to my everyday life. I would have rather read a novel by Dostoyevsky or a philosophical essay by Camus that spoke directly to the human condition. I only began to be interested in science when I realized that it was, in fact, all about *me*. The law of gravity tries to explain what holds *me* on this planet; photosynthesis is the process that grows the fuel that powers *my* life; the complex web of neurons in the brain are what create *my* experience.*

I now keep a file in my computer just for science information, and almost every day I make another entry, often returning later to speculate on what it means. I'm especially drawn to the scientific discoveries that point to *annica*, *dukkha*, or *anatta*, the Buddha's three characteristics of existence, and occasionally I will read about a research project or even find a single fact that sends me into an altered state, a revelation of non-duality, a feeling of self-liberation. Some science information I just find whimsical or funny.

Here are a few entries from my science file, with my comments and musings.

---

* I also find it notable that my interest in science coincided with the beginnings of my meditation practice.

Numerology

I recently read that there are 100 sextillion stars in the universe. Sure. I'll go along with that. Some astronomers must have counted them.

Modern science keeps presenting us with these enormous numbers, but most of them are meaningless in the sense of being incomprehensible to our tiny little brains and even tinier perspectives. I've now got so many of these gigantic numbers in my head that I get confused when I'm not near my notes, about whether there are an estimated 50 or 100 billion galaxies, and whether there are 50 or 100 trillion cells, and sometimes I confuse the two categories. Maybe we will discover that there are exactly as many galaxies in the universe as there are cells in our bodies, and that will either be a strange coincidence or a hint that reality isn't just random chaos bumping into itself.

As science presents us with all of these big numbers, it's becoming more and more convenient to be a mystic, and just see it all as "one." Of course, the essential question remains, "Who's counting?"

Yuckology

A few important facts to know about laughter. Research shows that when you have a belly laugh, you breathe in six times more oxygen than normal. Some experts estimate that twenty seconds of laughter is equal to twenty minutes of cardiovascular exercise. Usually something is funny as well, which is its own reward. In fact, laughter stimulates euphoria centers in the brain, the same ones that light up over chocolate or sex.

Scientific studies have been done on "the vocalization and burst rates" of laughter, finding that, across cultures, the most constant consonant of laughter is "h." Most of us go "ha ha," or "hee hee," "ho ho," or "heh heh." The researchers also found that nobody laughs with mixed consonants, as in "ha, fa, la, ca, kee, po . . ."

Anthropologists now believe that the human "ha-ha" evolved from the rhythmic sound made by other primate species when tickling and chasing each other in play. They make a sound like "hooh hooh."

Primates like to tickle each other, and one scientist has determined that the first joke ever made was the fake tickle, when the gesture to tickle is made but withdrawn before contact. "Ha ha. Fooled you."

✳ ✳ ✳ ✳ ✳

More numbers. Every cell in your body goes through four thousand transactions a second—processing fuels, exchanging chemical and electrical signals with other cells, monitoring the environment, creating proteins and enzymes. Considering that you have approximately 50 trillion cells in your body, there are literally quadrillions of events taking place inside of you every single second. Stay mindful!

Neurology

I love the new neuroscience, especially when it confirms my meditation experience. But sometimes I sense that the science information is bringing a bias into my spiritual practice. For instance, ever since I heard that greater activity in the left anterior region of the brain correlates with more contentment, I've been sort of "leaning" that way in meditation, exploring that area of my head with my attention. When I first started to meditate I would often focus on the pressure around my "third eye," until my teacher Goenka told me to stop because it would lead to the yogic powers known as *siddhis*, and then I'd be seduced from the pure path of the Buddha.

But I'm going to let myself do a little more exploration of that left anterior region. If I find the sweet spot I'll let you know.

It's a Gas

Scientists say that the convulsions of the early universe created vast amounts of hydrogen and helium, and now the entire cosmos is filled with those gases. If there is *helium* everywhere, my voice could actually be an octave or so lower than it sounds. There's a good chance that none of us have heard our *true* voices.

Climatology, Anthropology, Whatever

Global warming is a big problem for modern humanity, but our ancestors would have welcomed it. Just fifty thousand years ago, glaciers covered the land masses of Europe and North America all year round. There wasn't even a season worthy of the name "summer," which was only invented a few millennia ago, presumably by the "Summerians." They also figured out that when the sun gets hot, it's a good time for plants to grow, and this led directly to the invention of agriculture, civilization, and mint-flavored iced tea.

But for many thousands of years it was soooo cold on planet earth that people even prayed to the sun, like in Egypt, where they worshiped the sun god. (That religion, no doubt, was the origin of the chant, "Rah, Rah, Rah.")

Now we're worried that it's getting too hot. And we've discovered that human activity is one main reason for the heat. Simply put, we are starting to cook ourselves. If greenhouse gases increase too much we will be poached. But if the ozone layer disappears first we will be microwaved. Would you like fries with that?

This global warming problem is another sign of the human inability to understand the law of karma. It should have been more obvious. In just the last hundred years or so, humans have burned up *millions* of years worth of the sun's stored energy. Currently, every single day we burn an estimated 50 million barrels of oil—that's a huge lake full of oil—set afire every day.

The threat of global warming is at least bringing our attention to the fact that we live in an atmosphere. As we watch the temperature rising, we are also reminded that we are now living through a very benign climatic era. The birth of agriculture arrived at the end of an ice age, and since only about ten thousand years ago we've been able to feed ourselves and still have plenty of time and energy left over to do things like invent automobiles and stoves, and learn how to meditate. Some gratitude is in order.

Now global warming will be a test of our smarts and tool-making ability. Can science come to our rescue and turn down the planetary thermostat?

According to a 2007 story in the *New York Times*,

engineers are now coming up with ways to stop or miti-gate global warming—mostly schemes to deflect the sun's rays. One idea is to put millions of reflecting lenses into orbit in order to bend sunlight away from earth. It would be like putting sunglasses on the planet. From outer space it would look like the earth was making a fashion statement.

Another solution being proposed—and I'm not making this up—is to float white plastic or white foam disks across great stretches of the ocean; again, to deflect the sun's light and heat. I don't know, but maybe we should consult with the dolphins first. A similar plan proposes to cover vast areas of the deserts with white plastic mulch. But we already tried that—it's called Los Angeles.

Why not just have the government pave the streets with gold . . . literally? This would reflect the sun's rays back into space and at the same time make good on the fantasies about America.

Of course, the obvious solution is to cut back on our carbon consumption. But we're made out of carbon! Are we getting too fat on the stuff? Is that why our carbon footprint is so wide and deep? Maybe its time for humanity to go on a low carb-on diet.

When I hear about the issue of global warming I often think of the Buddha's fire sermon, where he declares that everything is burning. In fact, nirvana means "no fires." The spiritual path is the gradual dampening of desire, the extinquishing of greed, hatred, and delusion. Maybe meditation is exactly what humanity needs more than anything right now. It's time to chill.

Astrophysics, Evolution, and Buddhology

As you may have heard, we can no longer regard space or time as separate dimensions. They are as inseparable as up and down, light and dark, right sock and left sock. Time and space are now spacetime. *Where* you are is also *when*.*

---

* Spiritual seekers might want to take note, that if spacetime is a single dimension, then "be here now" is redundant.

Meanwhile, the mind-body split persists. Prominent modern pundits and spiritual adepts still proclaim that we are born through a spiritual medium as opposed to a physical one, and they insist that our essence has nothing to do with flesh and bones.

But what if both matter *and* spirit are necessary for our existence? Perhaps they are as inseparable as space and time (spacetime) and are both are required for our soul or consciousness to manifest. This is an era of conjunctions; of everything being "entangled," as the physicists put it. So maybe we could think of ourselves as spiritmatter, or better yet, spiritstuff. The right stuff.

Darwin Admits Crime!

In his secret notebooks, Darwin commented that beginning to write about his ideas was "like confessing a murder." Yes, Sir Charles, and the murder victim is the collective human ego that sets us apart from other forms of life, when in fact we are composed of them and shaped by them. They are alive in us now. That's an entire worldview you had in your sights, Charlie, and you hit it! It's dying now, but very slowly.

The Fact of the Matter

If all the actual "matter" of all of the 6 billion people on earth were condensed into a single solid lump, we would all make up the size of a sugar cube. Sweet, but it doesn't amount to much.

DNA by the Numbers

One of my favorite science statistics is this: if the strands of DNA inside your body were stretched out end to end, they would go around the earth millions of times. That fact conveys a sense of the enormous size of the instruction manual necessary for building and maintaining you—the blueprints for eyes, liver, brain stem, muscles, toenails, the whole works—plus the settings and directions that keep all the parts doing their jobs.

Consider the numbers: you are composed of an estimated 50 to 100 trillion cells. Each cell is millions of times smaller than a pinhead, and yet inside each of them is a drop of seawater, and floating in that miniature ocean is a *two-yard* long strand of DNA, wrapped millions of times around itself.

The reason so much DNA can be contained inside the minuscule cell body is that DNA is so narrow—only a couple of molecules in width, making it a *billion* times longer than it is wide, and much too narrow to be perceived by the most powerful microscopes. So two yards of DNA manages to fit inside each of your trillions of cells and—the statistics are hard to believe—some scientists estimate that the DNA inside of you is 125 billion miles long.

Equally astonishing is that the two yards of DNA in each of your cells contains the same amount of information as 1,500 encyclopedia volumes. In some real sense, all of the lessons that life has ever learned are stored inside of you. You are a walking biology archive, a living library of life on earth.

The genetic code created through DNA is often compared to a great book, essentially the story of life written out in chemicals. The author of the book is Nature, writing over a very long period of time, at the rate of a few single letters every few millennia, always revising, refining, remaking the shape and function of living beings, producing all the millions of different instruction manuals for life on earth. The manual for you and me is so complex we're just lucky we don't have to put ourselves together by ourselves.

Sub-Subatomic Physics

I read in some Buddhist literature (probably the *Abhidhamma*) that the Buddha experienced things changing millions of times in the blink of an eye. (Did he slow down his mind enough to count the changes?)

Meanwhile, inside the subatomic world we find evidence of an impermanence that is so impermanent it makes our ordinary reality seem frozen in time. Way down inside of everything, where the quarks are doing a line-dance inside of an electron, events are occurring in increments far shorter than the blink of an eye (considered to be one-tenth of a second). In the subatomic world, time is sometimes measured in what scientists have named "attoseconds"—a millionth of a trillionth of a second. It takes an electron about an attosecond to travel all the way around a proton.

Meanwhile, inside the proton, perhaps one level deeper into reality, an attosecond would be regarded as a long nap. Down here time is measured in zeptoseconds—a *billionth* of a trillionth of a second. Before you can even blink—Zepto!—it's gone.

I think at some point the physicists realized that they had entered a Marx Brothers routine, where the jokes are coming so fast you begin to see that it's all a joke. So when they started to measure things changing even faster—in trillionths of a trillionth of a second— they named it a "yoctosecond." Atto, zepto, and yockto. "Hello, I must be going."

By the way, the time it takes for a quark to go around a proton is somewhere between a zeptosecond and a yocktosecond.

All you can do is smile, and let go.

9

A Fool's Paradise

"What, me worry?"

ALFRED E. NEUMAN

Strange as it may seem, I like to think of myself as a fool. Not only do I believe it to be an accurate designation, but a liberating one. Once I embrace my essential foolish nature, I no longer have to pretend to be efficient, successful, wise, or compassionate. I can just be me, someone a little weak of will, usually caught up in the mundane dramas of my life and times. As a fool, I no longer have to struggle so much against myself and the way things are, striving to turn water into wine. I also take comfort in the observation of the Taoist rascal Chuang Tzu, who says, "Those who know they are fools, are not the biggest fools."

A simple exercise in foolish realism is to look at yourself in the mirror, not with an eye to grooming, but with an eye to seeing who's there. First check out your personality, "Give us a smile, then. And how about one of those looks of *gravitas* that you can put on at a minute's notice? Try the sly come-hither glance, the one that you use for seduction. And how about the look of sincere interest that Dale Carnegie recommended for winning friends and influencing people?"

Whenever I look at my various guises and masks— the ones that I usually slip on and off automatically without any awareness of what I'm doing—I almost always start to laugh.

Then I look beneath the personality and check out the self-conscious primate, not that far from the jungle really, driven by barely conscious instincts and trying hard to walk around on two legs and still look cool. Then I look even closer and notice the outline of my skull, waiting to make its appearance as bone, once the wind blows my face away.

Foolishness goes hand in hand with me through life. I had to laugh at myself during a recent meditation retreat after reflecting on the irony of what I was doing, sitting on my zafu. I realized that I had spent the first half of my life in school developing the ability to think, and now I was spending the second half of my life learning how to ignore my thinking. What was I thinking?

I also remembered that as a teenager I tried to cultivate a personality that would make people like me. After having built one (or at least dressing up the one I was born with) and walking around with it on display for half a lifetime, in the past few decades I have spent considerable time trying to dis-identify with that personality. I say to myself in meditation, "That's not *me*! He's always babbling. And he's such a fake!"

I long ago convinced myself of my own foolishness, but if there is anything I've learned from meditation it is not to take myself too personally. *I am not my fault.* What it comes down to is that I am mostly foolish just because I'm human, and the truth is that we are a species of fools.

Looking back through history we find that every few centuries all that we know about the world gets overturned, and yet we continue to believe that our latest facts and stories are the final word. Once upon a time everybody *knew* that the earth was flat and stationary. And how many humans prayed fervently to Isis or Zeus or Jupiter with the unshakable faith that these gods not only existed, but cared deeply about us? And although now it seems so obvious, it took many thousands of years of self-consciousness and overweening pride before a few of us looked at the apes and asked, "Could we possibly be related?"

* * * * *

Our biggest mistake, however, and really, the only thing that makes us into fools, is that we don't acknowledge our foolishness. We go around claiming we are highly rational, quite advanced really, noble and brilliant. And although our high self-regard may have some evolutionary benefits, it is also a primary cause of our stress and guilt. If only we would admit that we are fools, then all is forgiven. By definition, we can do no wrong.

So, let's celebrate our foolishness. I suggest that we get together in large groups and hold "fools' confessions," where we admit—out loud and in liturgical fashion—that every truth we stumble on will probably be overturned; and that every god we imagine will likely be deposed by the next civilization's god idea; and that in the end, we will have to admit, along with the Firesign Theater, "Everything we know is wrong."

We could turn April Fool's Day into an important international holiday, and could even designate a "Fool's Day" once a month, on the full moon. Just imagine how good it would feel if we all got together regularly in large public gatherings and admitted that we don't know what the hell's going on here.

For our Fool's Day celebrations we will need some foolish rituals. How about a simultaneous, worldwide, six-billion-person kazoo concert? Everybody knows "Row, Row, Row Your Boat." A mass mooning of each other might also be appropriate, but it may be more than the collective psyche can stand.

A very simple Fool's Day ceremony that can be performed in local communities or with groups of friends is the Homer Simpson forehead-slapping ritual, accompanied by a loud, collective "D'oh!" This ritual is somewhat reminiscent of the one that Jews perform on Rosh Hashanah, when everybody beats their chest and confesses to everybody else that they have sinned. On Fool's Day we would beat our foreheads and confess our foolishness.

Let's practice. Just spread out your palm and get ready. Now, all of you who thought that once the Democrats (Republicans) took over the government things would get much better—slap your forehead and say "D'oh!" Okay, everybody who thought that computers would increase political activism and bring everybody closer together—slap that forehead and let's hear a loud "D'oh!" Now everybody who thought that wearing crystals or meditating would solve all their problems, slap it right on your Third Eye and say, "D'oh!" Okay, one more time, everybody who still thinks that someday they will get it together . . . "D'oh!"

Embracing our foolishness, whether collectively or individually, is a practice of liberation. Don't think of it as defeat, or in any way demeaning or mean-spirited, but rather as a bemused acceptance of our predicament. On the fool's path (headed for the edge of the cliff, of course) you are free to stick out your tongue at the gods, let your hair grow wild, speak in rhyme, and stumble along without any idea of where you are going. Feel the freedom? It's a fool's paradise, and at the very least, you are fool enough to know it.

10

Busy Dying

"Death is just infinity closing in."
JORGE LUIS BORGES

I can see it all around me: people of my generation are growing old. And while it should come as no surprise, the fact of aging may be especially hard for boomers to accept. For some reason, we believed that we could stay "forever young." After managing to have a decade or so of extended adolescence, maybe we expected an extra decade of middle age as well. (It does seem as though some of my friends have been going through a "mid-life" crisis for nearly thirty years.)

But alas, here I am, just in my mid-60's, and I'm already starting to feel my age. I guess I didn't really understand aging—not until I started doing it more often. Perhaps like most people, I didn't really understand aging until my body began to explain it to me.

First my eyes spoke up. "Mr. Nisker! We've just about seen enough. We're getting tired of gazing at beautiful sunsets, staring at women, and looking for lost socks in dark closets. And we're especially tired of all that reading you do, looking at those damn little squiggly black marks on the white background for hours at a time! At this age you aren't going to learn anything new anyway, so we've decided to kick back here in your head, relax the old receptors and focusing muscles, and go into semiretirement."

Around the same time, my bowels spoke up. They've been talking to me my whole life, but suddenly they started singing a different tune: "Mr. Nisker, we're tired of your crap! Tired of pushing it around down here—a couple of shit-loads a day! So we're going on a work slowdown. You used to take a newspaper into the toilet with you, but you'd better start taking a novel."

My bowels had obviously not consulted with my eyes.

Next my testicles started on a rant. "Okay, man! We've done a lot of hard work down here over the years. Probably produced enough sperm to populate an entire galaxy with your offspring. And we know you've wasted a lot of it, too—all those times when there wasn't an egg anywhere in the vicinity, but you just had to have another one of your sacrificial spasms. Well, maybe it's time to take those vows of celibacy, or else start seriously practicing tantra, because we're just about out of juice."

Moving on down, my knees gained courage from the other uprisings and began asking, "How many more steps, brother? How many more times do we have to fight gravity to move your rear end from one place to another in your endless search for meaningless pleasures? We've been on a treadmill down here and we're giving notice now—unless you slow down, we'll put you behind a walker before your time."

Then my bladder spoke to me. It was nice, and tried to explain: "Hey, Wes, you know how when you go over to the sink and turn on the faucet, and there's a washer broken? So the water comes out in a spray, or sideways. And you can't turn it *all* the way off. Well, we've got a broken washer down here, and we can't seem to find a replacement. So don't plan to get a full night's sleep again, at least not until your next life."

Of course my memory speaks to me a lot lately. It usually has only two words to say: "Forget it!"

✻ ✻ ✻ ✻ ✻

So, it is now becoming real to me: I am aging. And aging is nothing less than the process of dying. I don't think my death will be coming anytime soon, but I know that my body is getting tired, and my mind is losing interest in the pursuit of experiences, most of which are nothing but reruns. I could get stronger eyeglasses, drink prune juice, rub ointments on my joints and muscles, take tons of antioxidants plus all the herbs and vitamins that could possibly help revitalize my organs and lengthen the life of my cells, but there is no longer any hope for substantial improvements of the house in which I live.

And that's one good thing to be said for aging: it gets you ready for death.

Although I don't think my death is imminent, it could happen before I finish writing this book. You'll have to read on to find out if I make it or not. The uncertainty should at least create a little dramatic tension.

You, too, are going to die, dear reader, no matter how good homeland security becomes and in spite of all the wonders of modern medicine. You might even expire while reading the next sentence or two. Of course, I'm probably not the first to inform you of your inevitable fate, and therefore not responsible for scaring you to death. But even if you do survive this day, in a brief seventy years most of you reading this will be dead of some cause or another, and in one hundred years, it is unlikely that any of you will be around, at least not in this mind and body.

Of course, we all have been aging and dying since the day we were born. So why bring it up? Some of us are doing okay for now; quite alive, thank you. Why think about the finale?

One good reason, according to the sages, is that

contemplating death will teach us how to live. Gautama Buddha says, "Of all mindfulness meditations, that on death is supreme." If you can conquer the most primal of fears the rest is easy. In Zen they say, "Die before you die." Then, presumably, when death comes around you can say to it, "Been there, done that." And, as one African proverb puts it, "When death comes, may it find you alive."

Of course, it would be easier if I could believe that I won't die. Many humans have pulled off this great sleight-of-mind trick to save themselves from death. Somewhere, way back in time, our ancestors decided to became immortal by simply believing that death doesn't happen. Poof! That was easy.

Imagine way back when early humans first started to figure out the facts about death, and the elders called everybody together for an emergency meeting. "Well, it looks like it is going to happen to everyone! Plop. No more movement. No more breathing, talking, farting. Nothing! Even Joe, our revered leader and the smartest guy ever, fell over last week and now he's starting to stink."

So then the shamans got together to figure out what to do, and maybe they took some drugs or something, and what came to them—praise the lord—was an afterlife. They came back to the people and said, "Don't worry about death. There is some part of you—in fact, the really important part—and it's separate from your body, and it will go on forever. "Whoopie," the people shouted. "No death! Hopefully I'm headed off to nirvana or paradise where nothing can bother me. And even if I have to go through another life as a peasant or a dog, at least I will still be alive! Whew! That was close!"

In the West, most of us believe that we only get one life, and how we live it determines whether we will spend eternity in heaven or hell. What a burden it is to carry that assumption around! A belief in reincarnation would at least give us some slack; we would have many lifetimes to get it right.

But the Hindus and Buddhists do not view the idea of many lives as a blessing, because you have to go through the painful processes of birth and death over and over again. And if you think that life's a bitch and then you die, a belief in reincarnation means that life's a bitch and then you die, and then you're reborn, and then life's a bitch and then you die, etc. In the Hindu and Buddhist worldview, only after we have achieved complete spiritual realization do we become liberated from the tiresome cycle of births and deaths. But, of course, that makes the whole enterprise into a bum deal: once you master the game, it's all over!

Many people find it soothing to believe in an afterlife, but as a species we may no longer be able to afford the luxury. Our belief in an individual destiny beyond this life has lifted us too far out of our bodies and too far from concern for our *collective* survival; the continuance of what we might call "the world soul." If we can accept that our identity is intrinsically linked to our bodies, we will understand ourselves as part of the life of this planet; each of us a cell in the larger body of the living earth.

So we bow to death, the great teacher. The great equalizer. The one who wipes the slate clean. Even while alive, we are bowing to death: to the death of another year, to the death of this moment—there it went—and to the death of friends, ideas, projects, and even occasionally to the death of nation-states and civilizations as they come and go on the stage of human history. May they all rest in peace.

And when our turn comes, hopefully whatever wisdom we have gathered from living will bring us a kind of ease with the dissolution of name, rank, and serial number as well as the body that carried them around. Hopefully we will have gained a deep humility about who we are and what it all means. Hopefully we will go out with a deep bow, full of gratitude for the ride.

"Poem"
WHY I
MEDITATE

(After Allen Ginsberg)

I meditate because I suffer. I suffer therefore I am. I am, therefore I meditate.

I meditate because there are so many other things to do.

I meditate because when I was younger it was all the rage.

I meditate because Siddhartha Gautama, Bodhidharma, Marco Polo, the British Raj, Carl Jung, Alan Watts, Jack Kerouac, Alfred E. Neuman, et al.

I meditate because I have all the information I need.

I meditate because the largest colonies of living beings, the coral reefs, are dying.

I meditate because I want to touch into deep time,

where the history of humanity can be seen as just an evolutionary adjustment period.

I meditate because evolution gave me a big brain, but it didn't come with an instruction manual.

I meditate because life is too short and sitting slows it down.

I meditate because life is too long and I need an occasional break.

I meditate because I want to experience the world as Rumi did, or Walt Whitman, or as Mary Oliver does.

I meditate because now I know that enlightenment doesn't exist, so I can relax.

I meditate because of the Dalai Lama's laugh.

I meditate because there are too many advertisements in my head and I'm erasing all but the very best of them.

I meditate because the physicists say there may be 11 dimensions to reality, and I want to get a peek into a few more of them.

I meditate because I've discovered that my mind is a great toy and I like to play with it.

I meditate because I want to remember that I'm perfectly human.

Sometimes I meditate because my heart is breaking.

Sometimes I meditate so that my heart will break.

I meditate because a Vedanta master once told me that in Hindi my name, Nis-ker, means "non-doer."

I meditate because I'm growing old and want to become more comfortable with emptiness.

I meditate because Robert Thurman called it an "evolutionary sport," and I want to be on the home team.

I meditate because I'm composed of 100 trillion cells and from time to time I need to reassure them that we're all in this together.

I meditate because it's such a relief to spend time ignoring myself.

I meditate because my country spends more money on weapons than all other nations in the world combined. If I had more courage I'd probably immolate myself.

I meditate because I want to discover the fifth

Brahma-vihara, the Divine Abode of Awe, and then I'll go down in history as a great spiritual adept.

I meditate because I'm building myself a bigger and better perspective, and occasionally I need to add a new window.

The Evolution Sutra

There is no longer any doubt that the scientific story of evolution is true, at least among those who have a relatively large forebrain. So maybe now it's time to find the spiritual message in that story, embracing evolution as our new creation myth.

Besides, we are due for an upgrade of our metaphysics. Haven't we lived long enough believing that our essential self is somehow disconnected from this body, or atoms, or materiality, whatever that happens to be? Haven't we gone long enough believing that our purpose and salvation lie somewhere outside of the life we are now living?

Those beliefs are now dysfunctional. They take the divine away from the earth and place it in some other realm, robbing this life of its due reverence. Our major religions have come to regard earth as little more than a training planet, a place where we come to learn a few lessons, or burn off some karma, or get saved by some messiah or another. The general hope is that once we're done on this funky old sphere we can go off to a better place, where we truly belong, and be in another life living happily *ever* after. We will be going "home."

It would serve us better to bring our spiritual attention back to the earth. If we could feel ourselves as part of the life of this planet, we might take better care of our environment. If we bring our sense of the divine to this earthly existence, we might even find more joy in living, however briefly, here and now.

The story of evolution can offer us many of the gifts we traditionally seek from religion: it teaches humility, liberates us from our individual drama, and presents us with as much awe and wonder as any Bible. But the story still lies rusting in our neocortex. We need ways to make ritual around evolution; give it song and dance; internalize it. We need to mine evolution for its spiritual gold, learning our new role in the grand scheme of things.

So let's stop looking upward in prayer and gratitude for this or that, and instead direct our gaze downward at the earth and all around us, to celebrate Nature, the instrument of our creation, and the closest and most obvious source of all our gifts.

*"When modern ecologists and neo-pagans search for a symbol
for wholeness and health, they come back to the ancient goddess,
mother earth, mother nature, the Greek's Gaia. Only today
she starts as a 'hypothesis,' and must trickle down from her
rebirth as scientific postulate to become sacralized by the people's
shamans."*

THEODORE ROSZAK

Hello Earthling

The story of evolution tells us that we are part of the history of life on this planet, making our primary identity that of "earthling."* You can feel your earthling nature inside your body, which is composed of "all natural" earth ingredients. Just rub your upper and lower teeth together for a moment and feel the hardness of your bones. They are made out of minerals found in the earth—calcium, magnesium, sodium, potassium—all mysteriously molded together into your skeleton. Can you feel that you are a piece of earth walking on earth? It is though we are earth sprouts that somehow gained a lot of mobility.

Meanwhile, about 75 percent of your body is liquid, and most of that liquid has the same chemical consistency as the oceans. You literally sweat and cry seawater. It's as if we are drops of ocean that splashed up on shore and eventually walked away.

When you think about it, where else could our

---

* Of course, if we discover life in other galaxies we might have to become galaxy identified, which would make us Milky Wayans.

bodies have come from but the earth and its seas? We are all certified organic.

And not only are we made out of earth and ocean, we have been shaped by them. Your legs and feet, fingers and thumbs, this upright posture and big brain, even your instincts, emotions, and thoughts—all are the result of life adapting to elemental demands. Remember that for a couple billion years of life on this planet there were no legs or feet simply because there was no land to walk around on. So who needs feet?

As we consider our body, we might reflect on the fact that the most critical steps in its creation can be correlated with major environmental change. Scientists believe that upheavals of land masses nearly 600 million years ago triggered the "Cambrian Explosion"—also known as the "Big Birth"—biology's Big Bang—which marks the first appearance of many forms of life, including multicellular animals with skeletonlike structures. Vertebrates like you.

Over the course of three and a half billion years volcanoes erupted, continents bumped into each other, ice ages came and went, and life kept figuring out new ways to live, growing new appendages, plumage, camouflage, new ways of sensing, eating, and moving. Nature is the sculptor, carving and coaxing all life forms into being. Nature is the artist, and we are the art.

"Mountains' walking is just like human walking. Accordingly, do not doubt mountains' walking even though it does not look the same as human walking. You should penetrate these words. If you doubt mountains' walking, you do not know your own walking."

ZEN MASTER DOGEN, *THE MOUNTAINS AND WATERS SUTRA*

Geologic events have molded us. A meteor crashing to earth sixty-five million years ago has been linked to atmospheric changes that caused the extinction of the dinosaurs, enabling the subsequent evolution of larger mammals, present company included. The dinosaurs toppled over, and there we were, the ones who nurse their young—the hairy ones.

More recent geologic and atmospheric events are associated with the emergence of our species, *Homo sapiens.* The land mass of Africa, for instance, was dramatically altered by tectonic forces twelve to fifteen million years ago, producing the Great Rift Valley that erected an east–west barrier to the existing animal populations. As a result, the common ancestor of humans and apes was divided, and each group began evolving under different conditions. They got the jungle and we got the savannah.

Suddenly our human ancestors had no trees to live in or escape into, and boy, it must have been scary. The savannah is full of lions and tigers and hyenas ready to pounce and gobble you up, so you desperately try to see out over the grasses, but you really aren't tall enough. So what do you do? You stand up on two legs. Was bipedalism born out of fear? Nature is the mother of invention.

The ice ages are now recognized as a major force in the emergence of *Homo sapiens*. Scientists believe that our family of Hominidae came into existence during the colder weather of the late Miocene, seven million years ago, and our genus *Homo*, along with those of cattle and gazelles, came into existence during another cooling period two and one half million years ago, the late Pliocene. Our tremendous human energy and ingenuity may have a lot to do with the fact that we were cold. Consciousness and the opposable thumb may have originally been designed as tools for shoveling snow.

"We mankind, arose amidst the wandering of the ice and marched with it. We are in some sense shaped by it, as it has shaped the stones. Perhaps our very fondness for the building of stone alignments, dolmens, and pyramids reveals unconsciously an ancient heritage from the ice itself, the earth shaper."
LOREN EISELEY, *ALL THE STRANGE HOURS*

And just think of it, my earthling friends, here we are spinning around on the earth's axis at about 1,000 miles an hour. (That may explain a lot about life on earth—we are all dizzy!) Meanwhile, the earth is spinning around the sun at about 66,000 miles an hour, and the entire solar system is spinning though the Milky Way Galaxy at a million miles an hour toward a point in space that astronomers call the Great Attractor. Yea, baby! And everything attracted to the Great Attractor is moving at about 800,000 miles an hour toward a super cluster of galaxies called the Shapely Attractor. Whoa, earthlings, this mother ship Gaia is moving fast, spinning in several circles and soaring through the cosmos! And you don't even have to hold on!

Because the earth is holding on to you, like the dear mother she is, embracing you with her strong arms of gravity. Earth is the Milky Way's little biosphere project. The true "rock of ages." And it's everybody's 'hood.

So let's offer praise and reverence to the home planet by turning Earth Day into an international holiday. Maybe we could celebrate an "earth day" every month, during the full moon.(The moon is a celestial child of the earth, born out of her side. The moon now helps keep our oceans waving and our orbit stable.)

Proclaiming earth days should not be seen as just a call to "do something" to heal our damaged ecosystems, but rather a spiritual exercise, a time to celebrate life, regardless of kingdom, phyla, or species, regardless of color of skin, feathers, fur, flowers, leaves, or bark. Earth days will be a time to reflect on our connection to this planet; a time to embrace our basic identity as earthlings.

The Divine DNA

"There is a simple grandeur in this view of life with its powers of growth, assimilation, and reproduction, being originally breathed into matter under one or a few forms, and that while this, our planet has gone circling on according to fixed laws, and land and water, in a cycle of changes, have gone on replacing each other, so that from so simple an origin, through the process of gradual selection of infinitesimal changes, endless forms most beautiful and wonderful have been evolved."

CHARLES DARWIN, *ON THE ORIGIN OF SPECIES,*
THE FINAL PARAGRAPH

One of the most important lessons we can learn from evolution is that we are related to all that lives, and to all that has ever lived. Once we begin to include ourselves in the story we are no longer on an individual journey but have joined that grand procession of "endless forms most beautiful and wonderful." We are no longer the singular focus of creation and instead, we are one with creation. It's an excellent trade-off.

When we join the evolution story our family suddenly increases by a million, million fold. Almost as deep as being blood-related, we are all *cell*-related, and the proof is in the pudding, and in this case the pudding is the plasma, and inside of it lies the secret of all living things—the DNA.

Have you seen a strand of DNA? It looks like a slinky with a purpose. It would make an excellent religious symbol, with its two identical halves and elegant spiral shape: the logo of life. It is ready for the artists to adorn and embellish.

From the funkiest fungus to the most nothingness bacteria, to the ordinary grass that grows all around, to the great cats and big-brained humans, even the weeds and mosquitoes—all beings grow out of the information contained in the double-helix. This is the stuff that seems to separate life from non-life, the seed that turns ordinary matter into replicating plasma. It is the physical manifestation of *spiritus mundi:* the Holy Ghost, the eternal Tao.

As the seed substance of the entire biota, I think DNA deserves some spiritual attention. We could start with its name, "deoxyribonucleic acid," which is much too cold and clinical for this magic molecule.

So I have taken the liberty to create a new expansion of the acronym: I suggest that from now on, whenever you read or hear the three letters DNA, think "Divine Natural Abundance."

This Divine Natural Abundance carries with it a powerful new understanding of who we are in the scheme of things, both as a species and as individuals. As scientists unravel the genetic codes encrypted in DNA, we discover that we are not so particular and individual. Consider the fact that your personal DNA is 99.99 percent identical to the DNA of every other human being. In other words, the instructions for building and maintaining you are almost exactly the same as the instructions for building and maintaining me, the Dalai Lama, George Bush, Oprah, Julia Roberts, Jack the Ripper, and the Buddha. Our individual looks, personality and IQ are just a thin layer of paint over the basic human design. We are more than 99 percent the same. "Can't we all just get along?"

Meanwhile, over 98 percent of our DNA is the same as that of the great apes, and even more shocking is the fact that we share about 90 percent of our DNA with mice! But we don't have fur or tails, and not only can we run a maze, we can build one.

So why is our DNA so similar to mice? The answer is that it takes most of our DNA—that enormous library of information inside each of us—just to create a basic mammal. It took billions of years for nature to learn how to build a good skeletal structure, circulatory and nervous systems, and it is those designs that go to the core of who we are. We are citizens of a kingdom—the animal realm.

❋ ❋ ❋ ❋ ❋

"Descended from the apes! My dear, let us hope that it is not true, but if it is, let us pray that it will not become generally known."

WIFE OF THE BISHOP OF WOOSTER,
AFTER HEARING OF DARWIN'S THEORY OF
EVOLUTION.

The Victorians were shocked at Darwin's suggestion that we are related to apes, but they would faint dead away to hear that we share nearly 60 percent of our living instructions with worms. Indeed, we owe a lot to the worms of the world, who were the first creatures to develop spines: they virtually invented our phyla of vertebrates! And do we ever thank them? No, we put hooks through them and use them as bait.

The lesson in humility goes even deeper with the revelation that we share about 50 percent of our DNA with . . . yeast! Yes, the stuff that makes the dough rise. That discovery raises an important spiritual question for those who believe in an eternal soul—does the yeast also have a soul? Does each individual yeast *cell* have a soul? I mean, if we are going to declare ourselves divine, then what about the slime? And if we don't consider the slime divine, then where do we draw the line? Do mushrooms get a soul? How about mollusks? Daisies? Crab grass?

A T-shirt created by a bunch of scientists at the University of California conveys the same message: "We share 25% of our DNA with bananas. Get over yourself!"

Our species could certainly use some humility, but the message of DNA does not diminish us. It doesn't deny our divinity—just our *exclusive* divinity. Everything that lives contains the sacred seeds; we are all the result of Divine Natural Abundance.

Survive or Die

The story of evolution teaches us the laws by which we must live, and the first commandment is to stay alive. This is the number one imperative of every living being. Each of us has it, and every single one of the trillions of cells inside of us has it as well. And yet, the notion that we are driven by the survival instinct is traditionally cast as evil. As if you *should* be caring more about some DNA other than your own.

Thus it was that a storm of outrage followed the publication of Richard Dawkins's book *The Selfish Gene*, whose title sounds like a taunt to both the Bible thumpers and the humanists. But Dawkins was simply relating the findings of modern biologists, who tell us our behavior is largely governed by genes that only want to replicate themselves.

So don't blame yourself if most of your thoughts are about you. Even if your genes are selfish, it's not your fault. Blame it on your genes. It's evolution's fault. Nature seems to want it this way. And for good reason: Life had to be pumped up with the desire to live, down to the most basic molecules, or it might have died out at the first sign of hardship. If genes had not been selfish, the anaerobic bacteria that began to choke on their own waste might not have gone to the trouble to morph into beings who lived on oxygen. It was the selfish genes that kept life adapting, growing skeletons for protection, thumbs for holding on, words for sharing information.

Rather than cast the survival imperative as evil or brutish, we should celebrate it. If we consider all living beings as part of the same experiment, then the selfish gene can be seen as noble, glorious, even worthy of reverence. It is no longer regarded as selfish for its own sake, but for the sake of life itself. We should all be singing the praises of the selfish gene and toasting its insistence on living. "L'chaim!"

Your Mama Is a Germ

Why should we think that the universe was made for us? A better case can be made that the world was created for the lowly bacteria. Single-celled bacteria are the most successful of all life forms, having lasted for three and a half billion years, surviving all the great species extinctions and still thriving, uncountable trillions of them, teeming everywhere, covering everything. In fact, billions of bacteria are living their individual little lives inside your mouth right now. Maybe they even have houses in there, churches, and roads—a whole civilization between your cheeks! There is some speculation that bacteria invented humans as moving feedlots. Inside of us they get room and board as well as a tour of the neighborhood.

Whether or not they are the crown of creation, bacteria are incredibly successful, and one reason is that they reproduce by just dividing—they don't have to take each other out to dinner first. The little bacterium just pulls its DNA evenly across its body, and then splits itself into two.

Maybe to a bacterium that splitting-in-two behavior feels good, like sex, and that's why bacteria divide so often. Is it something akin to masturbation?

Too bad we humans can't go back to dividing as a means of reproduction. Of course, it would be traumatic to think of losing half of yourself, but on the other hand, dividing would double your chances for a happy life. And then quadruple them, etc. . . .

Another reason to believe that life was created for bacteria is the fact that they aren't programmed to grow old and die. Bacteria can be killed but they don't die naturally.

So the bacteria were doing quite fine for well over a billion and a half years, having a leisurely time floating around in the Archean seas. Then one fateful day (epoch), at some auspicious moment (era), the single-celled beings began to merge with each other and to combine their little packets of DNA.

You could blame it on love, but it was more likely a marriage of convenience. The merging of two cells usually took place when it was useful for the survival of both—"You've got a little flagella to move yourself around, and I'm growing some eyes, so let's get together and we'll be sittin' on top of the food chain!"

After some time, the cells that joined together became a whole new life-form, a multicelled being, who was now carrying information and instructions from two different DNA sources. Since two packets of Divine Natural Abundance are more inventive than one, the new microbes began incorporating other useful creatures into themselves and eventually had to start putting their overflowing library of DNA into a completely separate body. There was no more room in the cell.

So, "Ta-da!" Sex was invented as a way of putting great amounts of DNA together into a separate new organism, leaving lots of room for variation and complexity.

It must have been very exciting for the first few couples, suddenly discovering those thrilling sensations of having sex. And try to imagine two proud microbes, mama and papa—you've seen them on the Petri dish—looking at their little baby microbe saying, "Isn't it cute! Look at it twitch!"

But there was a catch, as usual. Once the mama and papa microbe got their DNA into a separate new body, it was no longer necessary for them to stick around forever. Their information had been passed on. (Life is information!) So the mama and papa microbe eventually became programmed to grow old and die. What happened, to put it bluntly, is that life traded sex for death.

Now there's a choice for you. Would you rather live forever without sex, or have sex and die? Of course the question is ridiculous, because we have no choice in the matter. It was only through a phenomenal number of DNA combinations, through sex, over the long course of biological history, that life grew into a being complex enough that it could even contemplate the choice, or begin to understand its own origins. In order to become the smart-ass creatures we are today we had to have both—sex and death. (Not to mention the fact that if there had been no death, earthlings would have run out of room a long time ago.)

At least now we know enough to acknowledge the bacteria and microbes as the parents of us all. And it's time to give them their props. Let's offer a deep bow to the smallest but not the least among us, the brilliant and innovative progenitors who invented sex, mobility, oxygen breathing—all sorts of fun things. BACTERIA! MICROBES! They were the first ones to be alive.

Past and Future Lives

The story of evolution gives new meaning to the old religious practice of ancestor worship. We now have a whole new batch of beings to bow down to and adore.

Of all our ancestors, perhaps most worthy of praise are the tiny mitochondria living inside each of your cells. These beings are the ones who learned how to transform the sun's energy into the energy of life, an act of genius that makes even our invention of language seem trivial. The mitochondria turned themselves into the batteries of living substances. The whole show runs at their mercy. Without mitochondria life would run down and out, period. End of story.

In order to keep the story going, many species of

life have had to overcome tremendous obstacles. Just imagine how hard it was for the first amphibians trying to make the difficult transition from water to land. "That's one giant leap for all kinds of life." We owe a tremendous amount of gratitude to the frogs, and yet they are now disappearing under the deluge of our human explosion.

We should also be on our knees to the wormlike marine creatures who first developed a skeleton: a spine, a segmented body and a jaw, praised be, the better to eat with, my dear.

There are countless instances of great invention through the eons, along with an incalculable amount of pain and suffering, with 99 percent of all the species that ever lived now extinct, having given their lives for the sake of life. We should be offering thanks every day at the ancestral altar.*

---

* As part of our ancestor worship, I think that when another species of life is officially declared extinct we should hold a public ceremony: a going-away party. Maybe we could put up a statue somewhere of a member of the extinct species, maybe even create a whole theme park of extinct species: The Zoo-zeum. "Now you can only see 'um, at the Zoo-zeum."

In the story of evolution we also have ample support for the ancient belief in reincarnation. The emergence of new species, with new methods of locomotion, perception, or consciousness can be seen as our collective karma, as we take on form after form.

The idea of our past lives taking place as other species might seem to be stretching the point until you consider our individual development in the womb. Your life begins in the shape of an egg, a single cell, the form in which all life began. Once the egg is fertilized, the DNA code guides you through the entire history of life on earth, recapitulating phylogeny. The single cell becomes a multicellular sphere, then grows into a tubular wormlike body. The human embryo then begins to develop features that resemble those of amphibian frogs, reptilian turtles, and avian chickens. Even after you start to grow arms and legs you still look similar to the embryos of pigs and rabbits. All of this happens in the warm sea of the womb, and at birth you repeat the grand exodus from the ocean, arriving on land.

Under the evolutionary view of causality, our karma is collective. Each of us carries the primal instincts, the animal nature, the species-wide habits, the survival brain. Seeing this shared condition inside ourselves, we can better understand and empathize with each other and the rest of life. The story of evolution is everybody's autobiography.

"Never say higher or lower."
CHARLES DARWIN, FROM HIS SECRET
NOTEBOOKS

As for our future lives, we must assume that evolution does not end with us. Some might find it insulting to Mother Nature to suggest that we are the best she can do. I can imagine that someday a new branch of our genus will appear, calling itself *Homo sapiens sapiens sapiens sapiens,* and this new species will look upon us as we now look at great apes. They might even put some of us in a zoo, or do experiments to see if they can teach any of us how to stop talking.

Maybe future beings will have developed ways to self-transcend, to create bodies of light, or to at least tweak the genes so that everybody is fantastically good looking, smart, and witty. Nobody will get the heartbreak of psoriasis, or even fear death, and people will, at last, live happily ever after. Damn, maybe we were just born too soon. Oh well. Just consider your suffering a sacrifice for the future beings, the children of us all.

New Animal on the Block

"Drive all blames into one."
TIBETAN BUDDHIST SAYING

Friends, if you believe that you have sinned, or that you are seriously flawed as a human being, I am happy to tell you that salvation has arrived. Just place yourself in the story of evolution, dive into the big picture, the history of all life, and there you will see that no one among us is to blame for who we are. The story of evolution says you were created out of the shape-shifting stream of life as it danced with ever-changing earth conditions and natural phenomena. You did not choose to have your consciousness, your senses, or your instincts for love or self-preservation any more than you chose to have your thumbs. Can I get a witness? In the eyes of Mother Nature we are all forgiven! You are not your fault.

For one thing, we are all human beings, a very young species; a brand new kind of animal. By the way, I hope you aren't offended by being called an animal. Our eminent scientists classify us as animals for very good biological reasons, but most of us refuse the designation. You'll find evidence of our collective denial at any café or supermarket where there is a sign in the window saying, NO ANIMALS ALLOWED. We humans walk right in!

But we are a brand new kind of animal, an animal just figuring out that we are an animal. The body that you and I inherited broke away from the rest of our primate crowd only about five million years ago—just yesterday in biological time. That's when the Great Rift Valley was created in Africa and our ancestors had to swing down from the trees of the jungle to live in the tall grasses of the savannah. It must have been as difficult as first slithering out of the water to live on land many millions of years earlier.

Among those who began to hang out on the ground was an ape-woman the scientists have named "Lucy," considered to be the mother of us all. Can we therefore presume that the father of us all was "Ricky"?

After living on the ground for a while our ancestors began making crude stone tools, and became a subspecies of human called *Homo habilis*, or "handyman." We "handymen" started standing upright more often, probably to fix a leaky roof, and after a while we seemed to like it so much that we became what we now call *Homo erectus*, or "upright" humans. And we're not talking morality here: once we stood up we ushered in an era of full-frontal nudity. Four-legged animals don't have to worry about clothing because their private parts are hidden by their stance. Standing up put our sexual organs right out front for everyone to see, and no doubt this led directly to the invention of the loincloth.

Standing up not only brought us shame, it also brought us pride. I have a theory, fully uncorroborated, that the upright stance elevated our heads too far off the ground, and that's precisely when we started feeling remote from the earth. We also started looking down at other creatures. We thought the crawlers weren't as good as those who walk. Our upright stance may have also contributed to our belief that we came from some other realm. With our heads lifted high, we thought we were above it all.

Most important, according to evolutionary biologists, standing up seems to have triggered a rapid increase in brain size. You would expect the exact opposite to happen, and that standing up would cause our feet to swell instead. But that's not the case.

Here's the scientists' theory: Standing up left our hands free, and after a while we realized that we could use them to hold and manipulate objects. So we started using tools—spears, axes, chopsticks—and doing so required far more brain connections to coordinate the more precise movements of our hands and fingers. So a feedback loop was created: better hands, bigger brains, bigger brains, better hands. Pretty smart, Mother Nature. Worthy of a deep bow.

Standing upright also left our arms free to carry our

stuff around with us, and after a few million years we started migrating out of Africa. Nobody knows exactly why we left, but I suspect it was to look for Chinese food. At the time our brains were only half the size they are today, otherwise we would have been smart enough to just send out for Chinese food.

Anyway, we started wandering around the planet, and got caught in an ice age or two. That may be one reason our brains kept growing—we had to think hard and fast how to stay warm. Of course, it would have been easiest just to grow a heavy coat of fur, but at the time our brains just weren't big enough to figure that out. So instead of a fur coat we grew a bigger brain and learned how to make fire. Then we started huddling around that fire and telling stories about ourselves. Stories like this one about evolution.

The Kisser

"If we are here for any purpose at all (except for collating texts, running rivers and learning the stars), I suspect it is to entertain the rest of nature. We are a gang of sexy, primate clowns."
GARY SNYDER

In the early days of human speech it wasn't so easy to tell stories because our lips and tongue weren't coordinated enough to put a lot of sounds together. Back then it was basically "uh-huh" or "nuh-uh," and "yum" or "yuck." But we quickly got good at talking, and soon were saying things like "Let's get something to eat" and "Your place or mine?" Et cetera.

Scientists believe that talking—sharing information with each other, gossiping, telling stories, kvetching—contributed to another large increase in human brain size. Proof of the importance of language is the fact that a disproportionately large part of our brain is devoted to the movement of the tongue and lips.

Now we're so good at making coherent sounds that most of us do it without needing to think about where to place our tongue and lips. Just say something—like what you had for breakfast. You don't have to consciously decide to move your mouth from the "eh" shape to the "gg" shape to create the "egg" sound. It just comes out fully formed, the second you think it, understandable to anyone who knows what the sound means.

Words became so vital to our survival and dominance on the planet that nature has now installed in us a biological program for language. It is a built-in feature, and we are each born with the ability to put words together grammatically, the so-called "language instinct." We are born to yak.

An unintended consequence of having so much of our brain connected to the movement of our tongue and lips may be our love of kissing. The other primates don't go around kissing all the time, puckering their lips when they meet each other. The origin of kissing must be in those extra nerve endings that enable our language. I talk therefore I kiss.

Kissing, talking, telling stories—what a wise and lovable species we are! With this mouth I sing praises to Mother Nature for this mouth.

Humans Double-wise, Double Wise

Both talking and kissing led to further growth of our brain, until it began to outgrow its home inside our skull. Eventually we had no other choice than to grow ourselves a bigger head. It was mainly the top of our skull that grew, becoming rounded and dome-shaped in front. Probably none of you are old enough to remember the old "slope-head" model skull, with the steeply inclined forehead. Maybe you have a relative with that old-fashioned-style head.

Our current new dome-shaped skull not only changed the shape of our hats, it allowed us room to lodge a bigger brain, with a whole new area of cortex. It made space for the hot new *human* brain, high speed, fully loaded, with multiple giga-synaptic capability, rarin' to go.

So the die was cast, the stage was set, and about fifty thousand years ago, just a blink of a blink of an eye in biological time, our immediate ancestors, the Cro-Magnon people, appeared. They made jewelry and masks and had elaborate burial rituals, so it seems probable that the Cro-Magnon had begun to ask really big questions, like "What are we doing here?" "Is there an afterlife? And, if not can we invent one, quick?" They must have also been the first to ask, "Does this nose ring look good on me?"

The Cro-Magnon had developed a whole new kind of self-awareness. They had become what we now call *Homo sapiens sapiens*, or twice-wise humans. That label supposedly means that not only do we know, we also *know* that we know. However, it may be more accurate to interpret "twice wise" to mean that we need to hear something at least twice before we know it.

Even more important than their asking a lot of questions, the Cro-Magnon people must have been the first humans to display a sense of humor. They probably couldn't help but laugh when they saw the Neanderthals working with tools.

* * * * *

"Four billion years ago the earth was a hot barren rock, and now it can sing opera!"
COSMOLOGIST BRIAN SWIMME

When we see ourselves in the story of evolution we realize that our species has created a revolution in the life of this planet, having an impact similar to that of a great meteor or ice age. Only about twelve thousand years ago, a split-second in biological history, our ancestors discovered we could tame and cultivate grasses; the grain that we grew allowed our populations to flourish and then, in the past few millennia, explode upon the face of the earth. With our new powers and growing numbers we altered the physical landscapes of earth, bending rivers, moving mountains, carving canyons. We completely wired the planet with our electric toys, and shot our complex machines into orbit in space to help us build a global brain, and we began flying around and off the planet in our iron machines so often that someone watching from outer space might think that pieces of the earth were breaking off.

In the process of subduing the planet, we invented fantastic tools that multiply the range of our senses and the ability of our mind. We can now see to the edges of the universe and count billions of galaxies, and look deep inside of matter at the very structure of reality (which turns out to be nothing but light). We have access to almost all human cultures throughout history, and we can compare and share the knowledge and wisdom of all the tribes of our species.

Even more impressive, over the past two hundred years we have almost doubled the average human life span. In that same time period our activity in the world has been radically altered. Just a few generations ago, most of our ancestors were peasants, and now many of us are called upon to absorb hundreds of volumes of information in a lifetime, to operate complex machinery, and even to play new roles as men or women.

And yet, according to evolutionary scientists, biologically we have not changed. Apparently we are still using a very old brain, one that fit the needs of people in small tribes of hunter-gatherers. I guess that explains our addiction to shopping. If it's out there, you go get it.

Our hunter-gatherer brain may also help explain our territorial ways, and our current confusion in the modern world. But, considering how much we have changed the world and how quickly we have had to adapt to this world we created, I would say we are doing a damn good job of being human right now. Kudos to all of us!

I know, that last century was a rough one, with all the wars and environmental destruction. But there are signs that we are waking up to our condition, maybe in time to change our ways.

I take hope from the fact that only 2,500 years ago, a blink of a blink of an eye in biological time, we had Lao Tzu, Socrates, and the Buddha—consciousness waking up to itself. More recently we have had Darwin, Freud, Jung, Einstein, and Hubble, who can all be considered our contemporaries, drawing a whole new picture of who we are and how we figure in the scheme of things. It could be that we are witnessing a new phase in the experiment of life and consciousness. Maybe we will soon discover how to use our hearts and minds better, and find harmony with ourselves and the other forms of life on earth.

We have just started to tell our new story. And at the end of every chapter we can conjure hope by adding, "To be continued . . ."

Be
Here
Wow!

"One cannot help but be in awe when one contemplates the mysteries of eternity, of life, or of the marvelous structure of reality. It is enough if one tries merely to comprehend a little of this mystery every day. Never lose a holy curiosity."
ALBERT EINSTEIN

One of the best things about being human is to be able to wonder at ourselves and the world, and be stunned into silence by the unknowable mystery. This can happen when you walk into a forest, or first arrive at the mountaintop and see the vista, or step inside of certain cathedrals, or hear a great orchestra, or see a megacity unfolding below your approaching airplane. It is the experience of what Buddhists call "suchness" when you are no longer analyzing and judging the world through your self-filter, and suddenly everything appears in its full-blown strangeness, beyond comprehension yet touching an emotional core.

As a part-time advisor to the king, Lao Tzu said, "When the people lack a sense of awe, there will be trouble in the empire." That is one reason we should cultivate wonder whenever possible, and learn to drink deeply at the fountain of amazement. We might then become less insistent on rearranging the world: we won't need to consume so much in our endless search for satisfaction. As my teaching colleague Joanna Macy says, "Gratitude is the antidote to greed." The necessary new version of the American dream is not to get rich, but to realize that we are *already* rich.

The Awe Muscle

Often all it takes to arouse awe or appreciation is to reflect on the facts of life. I use an exercise I call "Be Here Wow!" that I consider a workout for your "awe muscle" (that's the one that makes your jaw drop open in amazement). If the exercise doesn't work for you, that's okay. Stay cynical for now. Sometimes you are just not in the mood to be amazed. But often a little reflection on the simple facts—like, say, your beating heart, a muscle that automatically flexes a few billion times in an average human life, pumping the necessary oxygen and nutrients through a circulatory system whose parts if laid end to end would stretch around the earth—can completely change your mood. A famous Hindu guru, Swami Muktananda, once told me that he didn't need to perform miracles, adding, "I just tell people to pay attention to the blood circulating through their body. What miracle could I do to match it?"

Modern science tells us of apparent miracles, inside and all around us, in the sky and in our blood. A picture from the Hubble Space Telescope shows a single galaxy that contains sixty million suns, while the evolutionary biologists tell us that life has evolved from a single-celled being to a human, an organism that contains sixty trillion cells, each cell holding enough information to fill thousands of encyclopedia volumes. My friends, your complexity astounds me.

Sometimes all it takes to arouse wonder is a little existential musing on the rarity of life itself. So far we know of nothing like it anywhere in the vastness of the universe, except for right here, on the surface of earth. And the odds against life as we know it happening (remember we are talking about you and me here) are literally and figuratively "astronomical." Multiple conditions had to come together in just the right mix, with the laws of nature firmly established—the forces of electromagnetism and gravity set at precisely the right strength, and every atomic particle having a certain spin and mass, and all of the ingredients in exactly the right proportion to each other. If any of the particles or forces had been the slightest bit different it would not have turned out like this. (Look around. See the world and feel yourself, both so finely calibrated.)

The very elements that went into making your body required exacting specifications. For instance, the carbon necessary for life happened only because of the existence of an unstable form of beryllium that was capable of combining with helium to produce the carbon nucleus. If beryllium contained three protons instead of four, or if helium had three instead of two, they would not have been attracted to each other, and as a result there would not be any carbon. Then where would you be, Mr. and Ms. carbon-based life form?

If the size of a neutron or proton were a fraction of a degree larger or smaller, or if the nuclear force holding atomic nuclei together or the electromagnetic force pulling them apart had been just a tiny bit different, then atoms would have collapsed or flown apart, and no elements such as oxygen would have been created. And then where would you be, Mr. and Ms. oxygen-breathing life form?

It's elementary, Watson.

When I can feel how impossible the odds are against *me* happening, a wave of amazement floods through my heart. I escape from the melodrama of my life and suddenly feel privileged to be standing here, conscious of my self and my improbability. Once I begin to realize that the stories the scientists are telling us are actually about *me*, I have a new source of both wonder and self-esteem.

A Perfect Planet

And here I am, living on a planet that seems to be made for me; for all of us. Life as we know it would not have been possible had the earth been the slightest bit smaller or larger in size, or just a bit closer or further from the sun. If the earth had been smaller, astrophysicists believe that the heat of the decaying radioactive elements at the core would have burned it up, long before life ever had a chance. If the earth's orbit had been only slightly closer to the sun, we might all be living at the poles, or living underground as moles. If earth's orbit had been a little farther from the sun we might all look like woolly mammoths and be huddled around the equator, lowing at the sun, trying to stay warm.

As far as we know, the only place that life exists in *any form* is right here on this narrow landing strip at the surface of the planet. The biologist E. O. Wilson wants you to imagine walking from the center of the earth outward toward the surface: for months you move through molten magma and mountains of rock, and then, a few hundred yards before you come to the earth's surface, you see some bacteria and microbes in the deep underground waters, tiny pieces of matter that seem to move themselves around. Finally you break through the earth's crust and you suddenly see a veritable explosion of moving, breathing, replicating life forms—micro-organisms, plants, and animals, millions of different species—all concentrated within these few vertical yards of space. A few minutes later into your planetary core-to-surface walk all of the life is gone, except for a few birds or people in airplanes.

We rarely see the profusion of life all around us. We see the large mammals, including birds; a few insects, usually the annoying ones who seek us out; and the flora that grows in our particular climate, the trees, grasses, flowers, and weeds. Hidden from our awareness, in nature's little nooks and crannies, is a world in miniature, where huge populations of beings are living out their tiny little lives.

Wilson illustrates this miniature world by having us picture a large beetle, an inch or so long, living on a tree, eating lichens and fungi. As it walks around the trunk of the tree, the big beetle is not aware of the small hollows in the bark beneath him. Inside those hollows lives another species of smaller beetles, existing in a different scale of space. The surface of the tree trunk seems a hundred times greater for the small beetles who may not visit much of the tree in their lifetime. Meanwhile, beneath the smaller beetle are still smaller crevices where patches of algae and fungi grow in spaces too narrow for even the small beetle to enter. Inside of those crevices are even smaller insects, such as armored mites that are less than a millimeter long. Finally, these tiniest of insects crawl over grains of dirt or sand upon which are growing colonies of ten or more species of bacteria.

Likewise, in the plumage of a bird is an entire eco-system, containing many different species of mites and microscopic organisms. These creatures are so small and localized that they will spend their entire life on one tiny part of the bird's feather. Different species of mites will live on the outer quill of a wing feather, on the vane of a body feather, or in the interior of a downy feather, and so on "through what to feather mites is the equivalent of a forest of trees and shrubs." A parrot that lives in Mexico is known to be host to as many as thirty distinct species of mites, with up to seven species occupying different regions of the same individual feather.

When we look around us, the variety of creatures that we see is an expression of life's number one imperative—keep living! In every blossom, thorn, leg, nostril, bite, feather, leaf, call, color, etc., each being is expressing the ways it has found to keep its genetic information alive. Our looks and behavior are all means of survival, and judging from the proliferation of life we conclude that Nature is a determined and successful designer.

Take a Bow, Maestro

Evidence of Mother Nature's brilliance is as close as the nose on your face (or as near as your eyes and ears).

Do a little experiment: For a few moments bring attention to your sense of hearing. Listen to the sounds, and as you do remember that the world outside of your head is completely silent. Be aware that what is registering on your eardrum is nothing but vibrations of air: what we call "sound" and the experience of hearing itself are all created inside your head.

To aid in survival (the senses exist for that reason) life has evolved this amazing Rube Goldberg–like sound system so you can perceive events that happen some distance away from you. Something in the environment causes the air to move in particular patterns (air element), which then vibrate the drum of your ear in a certain way, which in turn rattles three small bones (earth element) that press against a fluid (water element) whose ripples vibrate another membrane that moves some tiny hairs that trigger nerve cells that send electrical signals (fire element) to the auditory center of the brain that produces what we call sound. (And the green grass grows all around, all around . . .)

Equal cause for wonder is how our brain not only turns the vibrations of air into sound, but also identifies the source of the vibrations (human voices speaking, wind moving through trees, engines humming) and translates it for us into useful information or even pleasure. Our natural sound system plucks meaning out of the air, along with thunder and the howling of wolves and the bad news on the radio, music, bird songs, and sweet nothings.

Art Lives!

There are other marvelous and hard-to-believe phenomena happening inside of you right now, and seeing is believing. Just look around, in any direction, and you will view a masterpiece, a work of three-dimensional art, painted by the greatest painter that ever lived—your eyes and brain.

As you look around reflect that what you are seeing is *not the original*. Your brain is creating a moment-to-moment repainting of the scene that enters through your eyes, a reasonable facsimile to be sure, but not the pure, unfiltered picture. The canvas that appears in your consciousness is being painted inside of your head, moment after moment. Move over, Michelangelo.

A glimpse of the painting process can be found by looking around with the understanding that there is no "color" in the world. Your eyes are adding all the pigments to the photons of light, filling in the hues, splashing your consciousness with color. There is speculation that color arose in the jungle, so that our ancestors could tell when the fruit was ripe and the flesh was rotten.

Remember, the eye itself is just a small piece of flesh, built entirely out of sugars, fats, water, and a little protein, yet it has millions of precisely calibrated moving parts. In the early human embryo, various groups of cells grow over time to arrange themselves in a coordinated fashion to create the eyeball, optic nerve, and visual cortex of the brain, as if they had somehow met and agreed in advance on the design and construction of the most sophisticated sensing instrument ever to emerge in nature.

The eye is an "instamatic," a camera for dummies. It can change focus in a fraction of a second, all the while adjusting for light and movement. Researchers say that the different muscle groups around the eyeball make up to ten thousand adjustments every day, putting out the energy equivalent to walking several miles.

The process of seeing is taking place inside of you at this very moment. Streams of photons are emanating from the letters on this page and striking the screen of your retina, which contains over a hundred million receptors or "seeing elements." If something moves across your field of vision certain receptors will register its motion, others will register the object's distance from you, while other receptors are so specialized that they will only be triggered by part of a human face. What gets sent to the visual cortex for processing is not a painting of what you are seeing. The light rays get turned into electrical pulses, which then get telegraphed along the million-fiber optic nerve to the primary visual cortex at the back of the brain. The electrical pulses are then sent to at least thirty other brain regions. What happens next is a brainwide conference call or group e-mail. Remember, during the process there is no "picture" being sent to the different parts of the brain, just electrical pulses. Some groups of cells will translate those pulses into a recognizable object or scene, others will locate it in relation to you, others will gauge its intention and whether the object is friend or foe, while other parts of the brain will begin preparing some response.

The image of the world that you eventually "see" in your mind's eye, the picture, is formed at the visual cortex, a layer of cells two millimeters thick on the back surface of the brain. The picture is like a map of the imprints on the retina, showing varying degrees of intensity of light. The signals from both eyes arrive at the cortex simultaneously, are processed separately, and then combined to give a sense of depth and distance.

Remember that "you" don't do any of this. As you look at these words, the process I am describing is taking place automatically. *You* are not transforming the light into electrical pulses, or directing them to different parts of the brain, or turning them into shapes and meaningful information. Evolution has designed the system and does most of the work for you.

Even the coolest, most objective of scientists are astonished by the phenomena of our eyes. As Charles

Darwin wrote: "To suppose that the eye . . . could have been formed by natural selection seems, I freely confess, absurd in the highest degree."

Was sight foreseen? Were the eyes built by some design? A seeing-eye god? The mystery remains opaque.

✱ ✱ ✱ ✱ ✱

By reflecting on our senses of hearing and seeing, we discover that each of us is a natural-born artist. As Alfred North Whitehead wrote: "The various qualities of the world are purely the creation of the mind. Nature always gets the credit which should in truth be reserved for ourselves: the rose for its scent; the nightingale for its song; and the sun for its radiance. The poets are entirely mistaken. They should address their lyrics to themselves."

We don't need to go to painting school or practice the piano for a million hours or knit our brow to find the right words of poesy. Through our senses we are creating symphonies, improvised jazz, and great painted masterpieces in every moment. (If you really want to boost your ego, go to the Sistine Chapel and realize that your brain is painting it for you.) Inside each of us is the artist, formerly known as god.

"The chief wonder of all . . . Wonder of wonders, though familiar even to boredom. So much with us that we forget it all our time. The eye sends . . . to the cell-and-fibre forest of the brain throughout the waking day continual rhythmic streams of tiny, individually evanescent, electrical potentials. This throbbing, streaming crowd of electrified shifting points in the sponge-work of the brain bears no obvious semblance in space-pattern, and even in temporal relation resembles but a little remotely the tiny two-dimensional upside-down picture of the outside world which the eye-ball paints on the beginnings of its nerve-fibres to the brain. But that little picture sets up an electrical storm. And that electrical storm so set up is one which affects a whole population of brain-cells. Electrical charges having in themselves not the faintest elements of the visual—having, for instance, nothing of 'distance,' 'right-side-upness,' nor 'vertical,' nor 'horizontal,' nor 'colour,' nor 'brightness,' nor 'shadow,' nor 'roundness,' nor 'squareness,' nor 'contour,' nor 'transparency,' nor 'opacity,' nor 'near,' nor 'far,' nor visual anything—[will] conjure up all of these. A shower of little electrical leaks conjures

up for me, when I look, the landscape; the castle on the height, or, when I look at him, my friend's face, and how distant he is from me they tell me. Taking their word for it, I go forward. . . . "

SIR CHARLES SHERRINGTON, *MAN AND HIS NATURE*

Brain Matters (The Gray Area?)

The miraculous is inside you at all times, as close as your latest thought. Turn your brain to regard your brain, and you will find a piece of protoplasm that is processing eleven million bits of information a second. It's doing that right now, and you hardly have to lift a finger!

Every second of your life the information is flooding in, millions of bits and pulses of data from inside of you and outside of you: from your liver and lungs signaling the condition of your bile and blood—"Breathe deeper, we need more oxygen in here"—"Temperature at 98.5 and holding steady"—"Low sugar alert! Get some food soon"—and from the sound and light show taking place all around you as far as the eye, nose, and ear can perceive—"Something small moving across the floor at five yards to the left"—"Unspecified motor noise heard, not in immediate vicinity"—every possible tidbit of data registering, most of it coming in beneath our conscious awareness that couldn't even think (*sic*) of handling this kind of volume, the incessant flow of data that keeps the organism up to the nanosecond on possible threats and opportunities, including volumes worth of extraneous junk that will only be discarded a few nanoseconds later, after all the information is sorted and reviewed by the brain.

The brain filters the eleven million bits of information per second through multiple review and control centers, holds a brainwide conference call, and decides what you need to know at this moment. It then flashes a snapshot of reality into your consciousness, and continues to do this moment after moment throughout your life. Not only that, your brain weaves the experience you are having into the ongoing story of you, turning all of the events of your life into a grand and meaningful drama, at least as far as you are concerned.

Most astonishing of all is that you don't even have to be there. The brain is a self-organizing system that requires no central director. In fact, the neuroscientists have come to the startling conclusion that inside of your brain there is nobody home.

The cover story of a recent issue of *Time* magazine reviewed the findings of cognitive science, with the headline "In Search of the Mind." Some people may have been surprised to hear that the mind was lost, and may have been more surprised to learn that even the scientists can't find it.

The last paragraph of the article states: "Despite our every instinct to the contrary, consciousness is not some entity inside the brain, that corresponds to 'self,' some kernel of awareness that runs the show. . . . After more than a century of looking for it, brain researchers have concluded that such a self simply does not exist."

The self does not exist!? This is not some esoteric Buddhist insight; this is science, as reported in *Time* magazine! Why wasn't there a nationwide panic? The "self" that we have come to believe in is a fiction; existential smoke and mirrors. Nature has constructed such an amazing brain that it can run this entire organism all by itself, and just to make sure we feel important, it also fools us into believing that we are in charge? This, my human friends, is your brain on evolution.

"The universe could so easily have remained lifeless and simple—just physics and chemistry; just the scattered dust of the cosmic explosion that gave birth to time and space. The fact that life evolved out of nearly nothing, some ten billion years after the universe evolved out of literally nothing—is a fact so staggering that I would be mad to attempt words to convey it properly. And even that is not the end of the matter. . . . Not only is life on this planet amazing, and deeply satisfying, to all whose senses have not become dulled by familiarity: the very fact that we have evolved the brain power to understand our evolutionary genesis redoubles the amazement and compounds the satisfaction."

RICHARD DAWKINS

✳ ✳ ✳ ✳ ✳

Just think, earthling: It has taken the universe 13.7 billion years to make you! A lot of work went into this being, and a lot of suffering and discarded designs and tinkering with particles and forces and sensory systems, and okay, so you are not perfect yet, but you are a piece of the universe that can wonder about itself and move around and say hello. That's a rare occurrence, at least in our neighborhood of the Milky Way. Rejoice!

"The chances of producing a human being through random chance in evolution would be like a hurricane blowing through a junk yard and creating a 747 airplane."
E. O. WILSON

* * * * *

After a little reflection on the story of evolution, I usually sit in meditation and feel my own existence. I feel my breath and the sensations in my body and know that I am a part of this grand show of life, which is now pulsing through my body. Suddenly, the whole mystery of creation is inside of me, and I feel intimate with all and everything. For a while, at least, my innocence is restored and my perception laced with a sense of wonder: What is breath? Sentience? Consciousness? Aliveness? These questions are koans, a means of pointing to the mystery; a way to be here, wow!

"O to have my life henceforth my poem of joys!"
WALT WHITMAN

ABOUT THE AUTHOR

Wes "Scoop" Nisker is a Buddhist meditation teacher, author, radio commentator, and performer. His best-selling books include *The Essential Crazy Wisdom; The Big Bang, The Buddha, and the Baby Boom;* and *Buddha's Nature.* He is also the founder and co-editor of the Buddhist journal *Inquiring Mind.* For the past fifteen years Wes has been leading his own retreats and workshops in Buddhist insight meditation and philosophy at venues internationally. He is an affiliate teacher at the Spirit Rock Meditation Center in Woodacre, California.

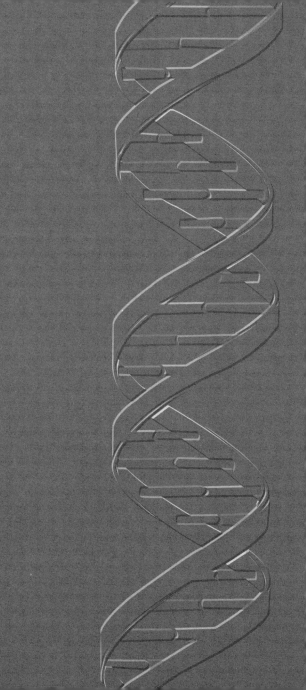

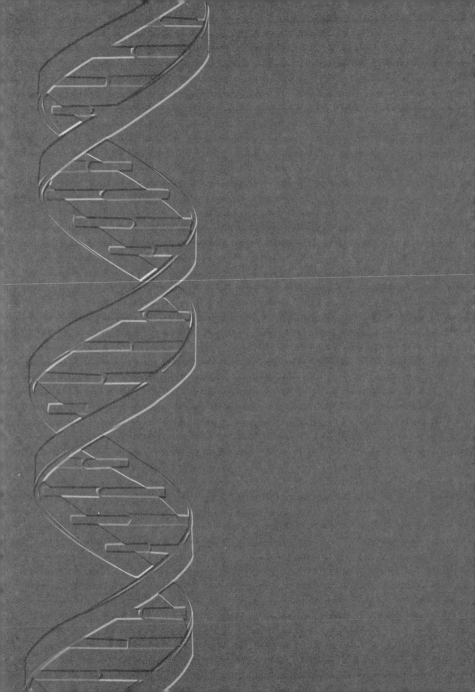